D1561650

ANATOMY OF THE PILGRIM EXPERIENCE

REFLECTIONS ON BEING A COVENANTER

ANATOMY OF THE PILGRIM EXPERIENCE

REFLECTIONS ON BEING A COVENANTER

Zenos E. Hawkinson

**Edited by Philip J. Anderson and
David E. Hawkinson**

COVENANT PUBLICATIONS
Chicago, Illinois

Anatomy of the Pilgrim Experience:
Reflections on Being a Covenanter
© 2000 Covenant Publications
3200 West Foster Avenue, Chicago, Illinois 60625
(773) 478-4676
All rights reserved

Printed in the United States of America

ISBN 910452-86-5

All Scripture quotations, unless otherwise indicated, are from the New Revised
Standard Version Bible, copyright © 1989 by the Division of Christian Education of
the National Council of Churches of Christ in the U.S.A. and are used by permission.
All rights reserved.

The poem "Portrait of a Cog" by Kenneth Fearing appeared in *New and Selected Poems*
(Bloomington: Indiana University Press, 1956), p 76.

Cover: *Emigrants Arriving in Göteborg,* by Geskel Saloman, 1872 oil painting, from the
Swedish Emigrant Institute, Växjö, Sweden.

00 01 02 03 04 05 06 07 08 09 5 4 3 2 1

Zenos E. Hawkinson
1925-1997

CONTENTS

Foreword .... *viii*

Preface .... *xiii*

I
ANATOMY OF THE PILGRIM EXPERIENCE

CHAPTER 1: Uprooting 3

CHAPTER 2: Planting 16

CHAPTER 3: Fencing 30

CHAPTER 4: Managing 47

CHAPTER 5: The Pilgrim Psalm 61

II
PIETISM AND THE COVENANT EXPERIENCE

CHAPTER 6: Reflections on Our Experience of Pietism 73

CHAPTER 7: The Covenant: Being 83

CHAPTER 8: God's Glory, Neighbor's Good 96

CHAPTER 9: What Did God Have in Mind? 105

CHAPTER 10: The Pietist Schoolman 111

III
FIRST QUESTIONS

CHAPTER 11: I Will Serve the Work 125

CHAPTER 12: He Satisfies Our Strength with Labor 129

CHAPTER 13: Little Serious Tension Exists between the
Christian and the World 135

CHAPTER 14: This Earth Is Not My Homeland 141

EPILOGUE

CHAPTER 15: A Statement about Myself to My Fellow Pilgrims 145

Foreword

This book is filled with storytelling. It is written especially for Covenanters. These stories about the origins and life of the Evangelical Covenant Church remind us of where we came from, the people who brought us to this present moment, and the many ways their experience has etched our own lives and identity. This vital link between memory and personal or corporate identity is an ancient concern. Even before Israel left Egypt, God required the people to remember what was about to happen to them, not once, but over and over. "This day shall be a day of remembrance for you. You shall celebrate it as a festival to the Lord; throughout your generations you shall observe it as a perpetual ordinance" (Exodus 12:14).

In his sermon preached at Arvada Covenant Church in Colorado (printed in this volume), Zenos Hawkinson reached back into that pivotal moment in the history of Israel and wondered about what connection it might have with our more recent experience. "And so it may be in our own history, for we too are a Passover people," he said. "Our fathers and mothers were uprooted by God's hand stirring in history, taken from the places where they had lived—they and their fathers before them for centuries beyond memory. . . . And if it is possible for the Lord God to move the children of Israel from Egypt, then it is possible for the Lord God to move the children of Europe to America."

I have often wondered, perhaps like many Jewish children, what difference it could possibly make to my life as a descendant of Swedish immigrants, that people I had never met crossed a sea so very long ago. It may be that God anchors the observance of the event to a commandment as a concession to our natural human forgetfulness. Would we remember on our own, without the imperative of the command? Is the command enough? If you have ever been to a Passover meal, you have tasted the special foods and observed the unique table manners which add an immeasurable richness to the whole experience, prompting the inquisitive child to ask: "Why is this night different from all other nights?"

We do not remember simply because we are ordered to. That is not how memory works. The story must be told again and again; it must be told well, and it must also be heard. The food and songs of the Passover meal conspire to release the imagination, filling the narration with vivid and breathless detail. The importance of listening to the story of Israel's escape from Egypt was written into the very order of the service and placed just before the great narration begins. Four kinds of listeners are presented. One of these listeners, the foolish person says, "What does this have to do with *me*? The Lord took *you* out of Israel, not *me*!" How, therefore, can we listen to anything if we begin with the assumption that it has nothing to do with us?

What do all of these old stories have to do with our lives? This is the question that this volume seeks to raise. We live in an entirely different world than that of our ancestors. The rocky soil of Sweden is not our soil. The Covenant Church is no longer the little Swedish enclave it once was. Some have argued that all this talk of the past, while quaint, prevents us from accepting and responding to the challenges of this new day. Moreover, all this talk of Swedish Pietism makes it more difficult for new pilgrims to feel at home among us. These are reasonable concerns. It is easy for memory to tumble into sentimentality and become trapped in nostalgia, blinding us from the new wonder God is performing in our midst.

While we must not become trapped in our past, neither can we escape it. Historians, among others, hold us to this truth. In 1959, Zenos wrote: "The never-ending fascination of history for me lies in the drama of human experience, in the strange repetitiveness of our situations and problems, as well as in the color and variety of the changes we experience."

My father was filled with a profoundly inquisitive nature, searching in every place for meaningful connections, weaving integrity into the human experience. He was at heart an historian and, according to his own self-understanding of that profession, a storyteller, working to improve and master the storyteller's art, so that remembering was a vivid, passionate, and often immediate experience. He wrote to his colleagues at North Park in 1976:

From the beginning of my work, I have believed that the first need of a dimensional human being is memory, living memory. It is a matter both of head and of heart. Without the head, we have mere anecdote, pleasant enough but without power. Without the heart, we have abstraction: power without context, a danger to humanity. Living memory begins when in some mysterious way, the deathly veil is drawn aside, allowing us to witness a life, now gone in its fullness. It is not enough to say, in passing, "these bones were once a man." The man himself must stand forth, like Lazarus from his tomb, before we can know what it is to be human. For the man himself is more than we can say about him, and to hold him in a living memory is to enlarge ourselves.

While fascinated by and at home in many historical epochs, my father devoted special attention to the great flood of people driven from the old world to the new during the nineteenth and early twentieth centuries. His files were filled with statistics, demographic shifts, lists of ethnic and national refugees who came from every corner of the European continent, spreading in great waves across our own boundless frontier, changing the American landscape forever.

Within this vast flood, he was most intrigued by those folk he knew best and loved most—the mothers, fathers, and children whose faith and experience gave birth, shape, and life to the Covenant Church. Zenos found that all the vast energies that erupted from the enormous shifting of populations were also present and at work in this little band of pilgrims. Their experience formed the themes that filled his reflection, his teaching and writing. He was convinced that these seismic historical forces were the work of God stirring up the pot, flinging nations about like dust in a great wind. But to what end? Or, as Zenos often asked: "What did God have in mind?" He knew, as a careful historian, that he would never be able to answer that question in any final way, partly because the story was still unfolding. For this reason, he felt in his bones, much like a command is felt, that telling the story and searching for the connection between memory and identity were central to all that is and is yet to come.

What does this have to do with us, the children of these folk and those more newly arrived pilgrims? Why should we even listen? What happens if we do not? These are questions we cannot ask only once. They are not themes that are absorbed once and for all and then placed on a shelf for interested archivists and scholars. Zenos believed passionately that the immigrant experience remains for us all; it is our most formative and lasting influence, one that we have only barely begun to understand. Indeed, the very process and energies that formed us continue to unfold in our present day. People continue to come, from even more distant places. They come without our invitation, following similar instincts to uproot and transplant. They bring with them their lives, traditions, and culture, which are transforming our communities and churches before our very eyes. So, these questions, while fascinating to historians and sociologists, are vital for us. The story must be told and it must also be heard.

We have divided this volume into three parts. Part one includes four lectures and a sermon presented to the Ministerium of the Midwest Conference of the Evangelical Covenant Church in Loveland, Colorado, in the spring of 1978. On this occasion, Zenos proposed a framework he called "Anatomy of the Pilgrim Experience." In these lectures, he separated four primary energies of the immigrant experience that he called uprooting, planting, fencing, and managing. Using this analysis, he urged us to see ourselves living within these same rhythms in our own individual, family, and corporate lives. The final sermon of this lecture series was rooted in Psalm 107, the song of the pilgrim. He found in these ancient words a source that shaped his reflection upon the whole immigrant experience and God's presence in it.

The second part presents five essays, published or delivered orally at various times, that represent my father's persistent probing into what might be called the heart of the Covenant tradition. What is it that really matters? What can we find within historic Pietism that may continue to provide essential nourishment for both identity and vision? Where are the deep soil for our roots and the well of living water for our thirst?

We have called the final section, "First Questions," a favorite phrase of my father's, indicating the important and enduring questions of life and faith. These are questions that cannot be finally answered, but need continual reflection, wrestling, and discussion. We have provided a selection of articles and some excerpts of unpublished writings that arose from within the experience of Zenos Hawkinson, the Pietist. You will discover throughout my father's work and life that integrity and wholeness are the underlying message of the good news. He found soulmates in the Pietist tradition, people who, like himself, struggled against the forces of fragmentation, which pull individuals and their communities apart in opposing directions. His writing often expressed the passion of the prophet. He was at odds with those powers, within himself and without, that seek to undermine wholeness. He was most insistent about the working life. You will find this in "I Will Serve the Work" and "He Satisfies Our Strength with Labor." In "Little Serious Tension Exists Between Christians and Their World," he responded to his old friend Irving Lambert with a powerful critique of contemporary piety. Here he explored the critical but often confused and conflicted relationship between clergy and laity.

The closing piece was written to his beloved community of colleagues at North Park University, the place where he taught for over four decades. He wrote this statement about himself in 1976, a time when life on campus seemed to drift into the doldrums. It was a season, in his judgment, when no one asked "first questions," when students seemed dull and uninterested, when the whole communal context seemed static. He wrote from deep within his own awareness of what makes a whole life. There is a restless spirit here, yearning for incarnation, a human life filled with the exuberance and wonder of God's presence. We have slightly reworded the title in order to address the reader, fellow pilgrims along the way.

We hope that the words of this passionate teller of stories, historian, and pilgrim will provoke thoughtful reflection within you, the reader, and discussion within the communities where you live and work—a full-hearted and thoughtful discussion! This, above all else, would bring joyful pleasure to the teacher in him. In 1959 he wrote: "What happens in the classroom, then, is a cross between a miracle and a failure. For all the strain of balance, I sometimes wonder who is really teaching and who is learning. Where things are often most alive, you learn something about the grace of God" (*The Covenant Companion*, September 1959).

DAVID E. HAWKINSON

Preface

In this book, it is a pleasure to make available the words of Zenos Hawkinson (1925-1997), whose life's work as a teacher of history and devout Christian touched generations of people in all walks of life. In these pages, those who knew him will once again hear his familiar voice and sense the directness of his personal presence and address. New generations of readers will also enter into conversation with one who speaks timelessly to what it means to be human, what the Christian journey universally entails, and what it means to be located in a particular denominational family where one's own history gets gathered up into a larger story.

A professor of history at North Park College from 1952 until his retirement in 1986, Zenos Hawkinson was always drawn to the great themes of history. With a broad-ranging curiosity, he used his probing into the particulars of each story to paint on a much larger canvas the drama that binds humanity together in a common experience. Born and raised in the Evangelical Covenant Church, the son and grandson of Swedish and Norwegian immigrants, he studied and told the stories of his own heritage as a way of understanding and connecting with what others had to say about themselves. He was particularly interested in the stories of people on the move, whether by conscious choice or having been swept along by the great forces of history, where one's authentic individuality, fashioned by these patterns, made a crucial difference to the formation and identity of communities.

The thread that runs through all the essays in this book is the pilgrim in relation to a community of pilgrims. Zenos Hawkinson's broad and diverse interests are woven tightly together throughout these pages. As a person of faith, the history of Israel and the history of the Church come alive. As a tinker and craftsman, his fascination with science, technology, and labor is omnipresent. As a student of human experience, his concern for anthropology, sociology, and psychology demonstrates not only his own learning, but his respect and admiration of colleagues who labored in other disciplines and shared their joys. As a lover of words, his knowledge of literature and the power of speech were tools of expression. His storytelling carried a certain homiletical quality, signifying that he was also a very special lay preacher. As a committed Covenanter, he embodied in his own way what was distinctive about this relatively young and tender planting in American religious life, and interpreted its growth into a maturing diversity for the sake of the present and the future. And as a life-long resident of the Windy City, though he traveled, he was much like Henry David Thoreau. He explored the world of history and ideas from his own polis, seated with a book or friends before the fire of his own hearth on Spaulding Avenue in Chicago.

The pilgrim image also says best what Zenos Hawkinson wanted to teach about human experience, including his own. It expresses the Christian life as a universal kind of experience, in which (as he says time and again) the pilgrim knows well the ground shaking beneath one's feet, physically and spiritually, and in it all God's sovereign and surprising humor in directing the flow of salvation history. Wholeness is achieved in a manner that is both global and intimately personal. There is also much value in the agrarian images of uprooting, planting, fencing, and managing, to which the most urban of people can still relate. At a time when a fascination with themes like planting and managing can easily become pragmatically and impersonally oriented toward outcomes, even polarized in relation to each other, this book is a reminder of the interrelation of these stages in human experience, especially when in service of the Church.

While some of the essays printed here were originally published elsewhere, most were delivered personally as lectures, addresses, or sermons. Since Zenos Hawkinson preferred to teach by speaking, much more so than by writing, it is all the more important for these pieces to be gathered together under a single cover. The first section, "Anatomy of the Pilgrim Experience," is based on transcriptions of tape-recorded lectures delivered in 1978, which were then edited and revised for a printed medium. In all cases, there has not been an effort editorially to remove or alter material that appears to be dated, such as when population statistics are provided or when the technology of the 1970s seems somewhat quaint in today's fast-moving world of the Internet. When reading the chapter on "Managing," for example, it is well to remember that Zenos Hawkinson was perhaps the most energetic and forward-looking faculty member at North Park in welcoming the computer age. His first computer was built from a kit at home. Each essay then must be read within its own context, but collectively their transcendent qualities are readily apparent as they address the experience of pilgrim, regardless of one's time and place in the story.

It is fitting that the publication of this book coincides with the seventy-fifth anniversary of the birth of Zenos Hawkinson. We are grateful for assistance from the Zenos E. Hawkinson Covenant Heritage Fund of North Park University. This is the first of many projects, enabled by the fund and the generosity of its many donors, which we trust will help connect the role of history to a meaningful present in the lives of Covenant people and congregations. In it we honor a faithful pilgrim whose companionship in life and whose enduring voice shed light on the ordering of our own steps.

Philip J. Anderson

I

ANATOMY OF THE PILGRIM EXPERIENCE

Our Father, we give you glad thanks for this unbelievable, imperishable, unmerited fellowship. Help us to continue to enjoy each other as we pasture in your meadows, in places that have been made available to us through your grace, because you love us—not because we earned it, but because you love us, because you are who you are. And help us thus to love each other even when we disagree, even when we see things differently, but understanding that we are sheep of the same shepherd, even our Lord Jesus Christ. Help that whatever is said or understood here may suffer the winnowing of your good sense, that what is good seed may fall into good ground, and what is nonsense may dry up quickly, blow away, and be forgotten. For we pray it in Jesus' name. Amen.

CHAPTER 1

Uprooting

I have chosen to divide "Anatomy of the Pilgrim Experience" into four parts that conclude with a meditation on Psalm107. While I am not entirely sure that there is an "anatomy of the pilgrim experience," there is no compelling reason to believe that there is not one. At the very least, I wish to propose for our consideration the possibility that we can see ourselves, at one point or another, under the four stages of "uprooting," "planting," "fencing," and "managing."

I am not at all proposing that these are mutually exclusive compartments, or that once you are in one you have nothing to do with another, or that everyone in the group is in one place. On the contrary, I want if possible to see if we can produce some liberating ideas out of the recognition that many of us are to be found in each of these four stages. One of the difficulties in sustaining an experience of "family," in church or society, is our mutual irritation with each other in the face of our refusal to recognize that some are in a managing role, while others are singing freely down the road like vagabonds in the stage of uprooting, carrying guitars and not bothering about bank accounts. While the vagabonds of the open road feel the freedom, the managers sit at home keeping careful accounts and have contempt poured on them as mere accountants, mere bookkeepers, mere maintainers of the institution. That is unfair, because presumably all the planting and all the fencing, and presumably all the dreams of the pilgrim on the road, were in anticipation of the day when there would be something to manage. It is ironic, then, to get there and discover that one did not want to be there at all. On the other hand, the manager, suffering from the persistent difficulties that go with managing (the ache in the shoulders at trying to hold things together, and the sense of panic and fatigue that go with uncompleted labor), longs with a sense of unrealistic nostalgia for the joys of the open road. It is remembered as a place and time of abandon and freedom, with no external responsibilities.

Those who plant often express contempt for those who fence. Building fences is frequently a thankless job, especially out in the high plains where there are not enough rails to cut for fences, and before somebody has invented barbed wire. To divide territories from each other is, of course, fundamentally to protect the plant. Likewise, if those who fence (because it is a necessity), have nothing but a kind of good-natured contempt for those who have planted, then something of the totality of the human experience is missed, which needs more to be understood than to be criticized. These are realities found in every period of history, not only among groups but with individuals as well. All of us experience, for a host of reasons, the inclination to uproot, even as we feel keenly the responsibilities of sensible management, careful fencing, and even occasionally the act of faith that goes with planting. This is not a simple, linear development.

There are two assumptions that shape my argument. I believe them to be defensible, in that they arise out of biblical and Christian experience. The first comes out of a passion for a sense of wholeness. The gospel—the good news—is that human beings have a right to consider that they were created to be whole people. It is human destiny, despite the interruptions of life in Adam's world and our own foolishness. Our true destiny is to be whole people; to be one single individual (paraphrasing Søren Kierkegaard); to be what we want to be, what we say we are, what we appear to be—in a kind of glorious inward harmony that gives us a feeling of appropriateness, destiny, good health, and joy.

In contrast, I feel (as we all must feel) the fragmentation of my daily experience in the present—as a citizen of America, as a citizen of the world, and as a member of the church—called upon and dragged, against my will, in a dozen different directions by different sets of values and by different responsibilities that require different sets of responses, different vocabularies, and all the rest. I do not deny that there is stimulation and challenge in the experience of trying to get oneself out of this fragmentation, but I for one am not going to be happy in heaven if it turns out that the kind of partiality, the kind of shallow piousness, and the kind of formulary pieties with which we are so often satisfied in our superficial relationships with each other are the rule in heaven. I would just as soon not be there. But I say that, confident that that is not the way in heaven, and that it will be, as C. S. Lewis remarked, a place where only very weighty things can survive. The only thing that can really be weighty is that which is really real, and our problem is to find a way to be at the same time God's people and *real* people. I associate realness with wholeness, even if this wholeness is marred by warts, even if, as the consequence of my wholeness, I am forced to confess to you that I am less than I ought to be. Therefore, I have to ask you by my very presence to understand that and to accept it—in fact, to demand that you accept it as a price of our fellowship as real men and women.

I can imagine situations in which it is not possible to be whole, and in which it may not even be desirable to be whole. That is, there must be some kind of wholenesses that are not good. To be wholly bad cannot be a New Testament ideal, but is it even possible to be wholly bad? If Lewis's vision is correct, that hell is a place much like Chicago—a gray city, marked chiefly by an absence of reality, an absence of weight, an absence of tangibility—then maybe there is no such thing as the wholly bad. Perhaps the bad soon turns out, as Augustine suspected, to be simply the absence of God, the total and irretrievable absence of God. Even in our fragmentation, then, we may feel within the internal conflicts of our life something that can be saved and something that is striving for fullness and completeness.

A second thing I am assuming—and it is an assumption that is related to the first—is that there is no good trying to escape our anthropology. That is, there is no such thing as a Christian expression that is not limited, at least in this world, by its time and by its culture. One of my colleagues has repeatedly reminded our first-year college students that "the same act in a different culture is a different act." That must be accepted, with all of its implications. Whatever may finally be true in God's heaven, where all things are run in a sensible way, on earth here our own views are inescapably relative to our own cultural experience and incorporation, even to the content and quality of our language. It is very difficult to express finally, in this world, an acceptable and defensible absolute, unless it is simply to raise one's hands in complete submission to God, to the Lord Jesus, to the Holy Spirit. But to attempt to define or express in word, song, art, theology, logic, or prayer an absolute divine truth unconditioned by culture, is, I think, quite clearly impossible. We are necessarily rooted in our past. We are necessarily in some ways the prisoners of our childhood, of the things that we first learned, of that about which we said, "Good," and of that about which it was said, "Uush." And, even at my age, I can still feel writhing around inside my belly the response that my mother taught me about things "good" and things "uush." One can argue for a kind of "deconditioning" that may occur within certain controlled environments, but I believe there are some conditioned reflexes that probably remain with us, at least this side of eternity. And there may not be any point trying to get rid of them, but there they are.

There is, therefore, no such thing as a church history that is not necessarily the history of the times in which real people are living. There is, therefore, no such thing as a theology that is not in some way speaking merely about the science of God, but also about the historical experience of the people who are doing the arguing. There is no such thing, therefore, as a church poetry, a liturgy, that must not necessarily relate itself to the daily experience of the people who practice it. My point is that it is one thing to reflect upon our history when we are in the planting stage, the period of abandon and freedom where a certain kind of liturgy may well be appropriate for the wandering pilgrim. It is another thing to arrange a liturgy for people who are managing space programs, major industrial components, computer technologies, and all the sophistication of the modern world, as though they were still footloose and unattached wanderers on the frontier. It is one thing to be a real child, but it is quite another thing to be a fake child. And if the church becomes an instrument of further fragmentation, then the church had better ask itself whether or not it is being faithful to the possibilities inherent in the good news to make people whole. That is why these four stages may be helpful to our understanding.

What is it, in the mystery of God, that uproots and brings people together in community, into a mutual relationship with one another? What explains the confluence of events and people that is the reality of the Covenant Church, be it on the congregational, regional, national, or international levels? Here, the uprooting precedes everything else. In so short a time have our lives become tangled together by massive forces over which we and our ancestors have had virtually no control, so that we might with equal truth say with the followers of Moses, "We were led by the hand of God into this wilderness." The British actor Peter Ustinov, son of an anti-Bolshevic father and a German mother, offered thanks in his autobiography to Europe for causing World War I and the Bolshevic Revolution because these great events on the world's stage brought his parents together such that he could even be born. Therefore, we are obliged to ask in reference to our own birthing as a church and people, why? How did this mystery happen? How did it work? And I want to respond that it worked because God did not merely shake the theology, intellectual categories, and the aesthetic perceptions of ordinary people in Europe. He shook the earth itself; he shook the earth on which they lived. The hammer blows of God, which sent fifty million people careening out of Europe between 1815 and 1930, have no parallel in human history, at least in the cycle for which we have any memory at all. Fifty million people! Forty million of these came to North America. The population of the United States of America in 1815 was about 8.5 million. With all the frontiers closed, where could such a massive migration of dislocated people go today?

Well, let us turn the matter around and look at it another way. Between 1840 and 1930 there left from Sweden alone—and Sweden's per capita rate of emigration was exceeded only by that of Ireland and Norway—about 1.25 million, mostly young people between the ages of fifteen and thirty-five. (Of these, about 20 percent would return to their homeland.) That is somewhat more than a fifth of the Swedish population in the middle 1860s, when severe famine and other push-and-pull forces began to affect a society under considerable stress in its transition to modernity. If one considers the present population of the United States to be about 220 million, in comparison more than 40 million would be leaving over the next six decades for other parts of the earth. That is staggering population movement.

Now, how does one account for it? What was happening? Well, we will never be completely sure, but our knowledge of the experience of the Swedish immigrants is full and rich because of the extensive studies of the past few decades. We know that new ideas had entered Swedish society, ideas that made it possible for peasants to work the land with greater independence and voice, and ordinary people to believe that they could feed their children with some regularity. Others came to hope that there could be an open future elsewhere, perhaps in the developing industrial cities and towns. Bishop Esias Tegnér, in a much-quoted, lyrical insight, said that the Swedish population grew enormously because of peace, pox (that is, vaccine for smallpox), and potatoes. Peace had prevailed since the early nineteenth century, because the Swedes simply stopped fighting when it dawned on them, as sensible people, that they were getting too small as a nation to have much success, and self-preservation could be pursued while avoiding war. Vaccines, developed in the mid-eighteenth century, had finally become widely accessible in Sweden, improving the infant mortality rate. Just as with the Irish, people who had nothing else to eat because of poverty or famine could eat potatoes, and the Swedes, as usual, made the best of it and decided they liked them. At least 700,000 people in Sweden became superfluous to Swedish agriculture because of population growth and bursting families on small, primitive farms. In addition, an ancient agrarian economy was being transformed by a modernizing agricultural revolution through which we are still going, placing enormous pressure in recent decades on the traditional American family farm, many operated for generations ironically by the descendants of Swedish immigrants.

To me, it is as a kind of statement of faith to recognize that when God wants to shake people up, he does so very powerfully, seldom with theological arguments, but much more often with experiences that touch the most sensitive nerves of all—the belly. He moves them out by directing the forces of history, as he may be moving us about now, if we only had the wisdom to perceive it. These Swedes were highly traditional, ordinary people, who did not necessarily get credit for imaginative and informed understanding of what was going on in the world. You get the impression when you read their letters, diaries, and memoirs, that what they were feeling was something coming to them through the soles of their feet, out of the earth: "We must move. We have no choice but to move. The world as it is here, now, no longer makes sense. There is no place for me."

Let us pause for a moment and reflect on the experiences in our own lives. Pastors are quite frequently faced with the question of moving or staying, sometimes quite simply because of the politics of their congregations, sometimes quite simply because they feel an opportunity and a challenge somewhere else, or because of any number of reasons. Others in the congregation may suddenly come to a day when their life no longer makes any sense as it is, not because of the church (at least, not necessarily because of the church), but because, in a combination of circumstances, they suddenly feel alien to their whole world. They no longer feel at home. They no longer feel that they have in their hands or available to them in their community the materials for a whole life.

They no longer have inside them the feeling of confidence in the future. Something has cut them off. It does not necessarily have to make sense to their friends; it may not even make sense to them. It may be—just as it was to the average Swedish peasant in the first part of the nineteenth century—a kind of instinct that flows into the feet through the earth, a kind of inward magnetism that turns the compass needle and points it west and says, "Move!"

There is no way to make this kind of understanding precise. We must recognize, however, that this does happen in individual as well as in general cultural life, and that it is not necessarily and always the enemy of good order. It may superficially appear to be the enemy of good order. A congregation has a good chair of the board of trustees who is suddenly called upon for employment reasons to move halfway across the country, and you say, "Well, aren't you ever going to put roots down?" Every family that hits the road sooner or later wonders, "Why are we on the road? Why aren't we where we were? How deep should the roots be? Why do we have this feeling of alienation?" I read in *The Covenant Companion* the list of pastoral changes and say, "Well, what in the world did she do that for? Why is he leaving? He just got there!" It reminds me of a classic conversation in the early annals of Covenant history. Hans Blom, the great old pioneer pastor, stuck down in Kansas, writes a letter to C. A. Björk up in Des Moines and says, "Dear Björk, I feel like a stone owl in the ruins." And Björk writes back, "Well, what are you doing down there in Kansas anyway? Why wasn't Iowa good enough for you?" No comfort—no comfort at all. But it turns out that Blom was where he belonged. At least, if the consequences of his ministry are to be measured in any reasonable way by the historian, Blom was where he belonged and Björk was where he belonged. The contemporary is not always the best judge.

What is it about uprooting? Except that, for some reason, God is not satisfied with the order as it is. We may really have done our best to get church life into a settled, stable, and regular order: we finally get a pianist who can play in four flats; we finally get the ushers to the point where they will not walk people in during the middle of the pastoral prayer; and people are finally standing up and sitting down together. In other words, having achieved a well-disciplined and orderly church, one must face the possibility that at precisely that moment God is saying, "I am going to bust it up because I have something else in mind." All that is within us argues for stabilization, order, decency, community relationships, and reliability—yet everything we picture as the body of the church in a regular, predictable way may at one point or another be vulnerable to God's disorder. The presence of disorder is not to be understood ipso facto as destructive, be it historically, theologically, liturgically, aesthetically, or communally.

And I find some comfort in that, because it seems to me that I am living in a world of increasing disorder. I find it perhaps because of advancing age. Whatever the reasons, I have a stronger and stronger sense of foreboding about the disorder within our culture, about the massive capacity of our culture to reduce people to a kind of chronic boredom, stimulus overkill, and hopelessness about the possibility of joy. From my perspective, this does not bode well for the future good of society. I find young people—larger and larger numbers of young people—who, at least at the present moment, have very grave difficulty staying with an idea for longer than fifteen seconds, or about the time it takes the television to switch from one scene to the next. The adolescent or the college-age attention span is very brief, partly as the consequence of the system of images in which they are now growing up.

But these are the complaints of an older man. I recognize that. I take comfort, however, in the possibility that this perceived disorder may in fact be the action of God blowing loose those things that I am holding on to. He may do so for the sake of creating a new and better order, for the sake of developing a family, as this Covenant family has been developed over time out of inconceivably dark and unhappy circumstances. And before you become too nostalgic about the joys of the good old days, just let me remind you what the good old days were like, when it was impossible to feed your children regularly. Read Vilhelm Moberg, whose well-known story of the immigrant experience describes a time when it was simply impossible to guarantee any kind of security for anybody without the most terrifying kind of worry.

I have become more aware of a dimension of the experiences of immigrants—not only the Swedish immigrant, but others from Europe as well. The naturally tendency, of course, is to stress the good results that eventuated within immigrant groups, but I began to ask why there were so many immigrants from across Europe and Scandinavia who never told their children or grandchildren where they came from. And you know what the answer is? Because they did not want them to know.

Because they were bitter about the Old World. Because they never wanted to have another thought about it. Because they saw it as a world from which to escape. Because they saw it as a place to which they never wanted their children or grandchildren to return. This can be documented in case after case. It is all very well for us now—after all these years, when the terrible casualties have long been forgotten and the wounds of separation have been healed—to sing in a mood of sentimental nostalgia the Swedish national anthem, *"Du gamla, du fria"* ("Thou Old, Thou Free"). But that is not the way the vast majority of first-generation immigrants felt about it. Instead, many sang "The Star-Spangled Banner" in their broken English and refused to have anything to do with the blue and the gold at all. And they had good reason for it. Here, they said, a person can walk straight and upright, without ever bowing to a noble or a priest. In America one is free. In the homeland one had been a slave to so many things and so many people. Whether that was universally true or not is not the major concern here. The point is that millions of people were moved about, whether they wanted to be or not. They had no real control over the process. That which we generally call "historical forces" overwhelmed them and simply projected them out wholesale. And we are their children.

Is there a reason, having been thus scattered, we are gathered together in this community? What are we doing here? What *is* our destiny? What did God have in mind? And one of our responses, of course, is that he had the Covenant in mind. To which a Lutheran friend of mind who listens to these arguments from me said, "God is certainly the least efficient workman in the history of the cosmos, to move forty million people around to build the Covenant." I guess there is a sense of disproportion in that notion. Of course, I was not arguing that that was all he did. But *at least* he did that.

Why the Covenant? Because one of the things that happens when people get uprooted, ripped out of one's old life, and when things fall apart, is that the old systems of security and relationships can no longer suffice. You can no longer be a farmer, you can no longer be a manager, you can no longer be a fencer. You have been ripped out, projected out, and you are a homeless wanderer. How do you live on the high road? You live by hunting and gathering. Sometimes that is known as stealing other people's apples. And how do hunters and gatherers live? They live in small groups, in primary fellowships, in what we call tribes. Show me a group of uprooted people, and I will show you tribes, unless, of course, they have become totally demoralized and destroyed. But if in the process of uprooting they have mercifully been allowed to discover just a few other pilgrims, they will become tribal. And what do I mean by tribal? I mean that their identifications are intensely personal and face-to-face, not at all in the abstract. They do not even need the written language. They live by addressing each other. They live by a set of unspoken rules, which they agree regulate their conduct. They live in daily interaction with each other, in small groups, and do not feel entirely comfortable until they are back with each other again.

Now, I appeal to those of you who have recently come into the Covenant family—and anyone who has been in it fewer than fifteen or twenty years can easily be made to feel that they have just come into the Covenant family. There was a man in my brother's church in Paxton, Illinois, years ago who, when asked to run for deacon, said, "No, I can't run for deacon. I'm just a newcomer." "How long have you been a member?" asked my brother Jim. "Twenty-seven years." That is what is meant by "tribal understandings." The same thing said by a member of the tribe is said by a person who is not a member of the tribe, and the one who is not a member of the tribe gets clobbered. The member of the tribe says, "Well, you know, everybody knows Johnson. Everybody knows Larson. That's the way Nelson talks. Everybody understands." The same act in a different culture is a different act. Inside the tribe, where the uprooted move within their own common understandings, there is the appearance of—and the reality of—security and mutual understanding. The fellowship can move, it travels, it is ambulatory, it can go from place to place. And elements within the fellowship can go from place to place, as Covenanters have, of course, time and time again discovered. The family is already there when you get there, like the two blackbirds sitting on the fence. If you try to get away from it in one place, the first thing you discover when you get to the new place is that it is there too.

Now, it is impossible to draw this picture with any sociological precision. One must ask the people who are inside it and know it. The tribe is appropriate behavior for people who no longer can make their living and feed their children by farming—planting, fencing, and managing. It is appropriate to people on the road, people who are uprooted. And when a person has been put on the road, either literally or figuratively, how can one survive apart from the tribe? Not unless one can turn to a movable fellowship, which expresses not merely the security of the moment, harbor against the rain, and a warm stove, but also (and more importantly) security within the cosmos. It is no accident that it was among the farmers that the piety cells, the conventicles, began to develop in nineteenth-century Swedish society. To them, the world made less and less sense. For centuries, the Church of Sweden, a state church, had been primarily responsible for ordering the lives of ordinary people. Its leaders, servants of the crown and persons of stature and station, were thought to have little sympathy for and understanding of the feelings of these people, whether it was their social pressures or their religious renewal. They represented a hierarchy set apart from common experience.

The peasants who felt in their bones that something was wrong and that they were being alienated, driven off their land and out of their ancient and traditional ways of life, could find little if any meaning in that formalized and legislated setting. And what is their response then? It is an instinctive response: they go to their tribe. They go to the pietistic cell and bring that which has already been forged in other places by John Wesley in England, and by the Halle Pietists and Count Nicholas Ludwig von Zinzendorf in Germany. They meet in the cell, doing the only thing that they really know, the only thing that seems to them legitimate, even though their activity violates the law: they read together the Bible, Martin Luther, and Johan Arndt. Out of this darkness, the individual has to have some sense of light, some assurance that the world is not totally absurd, that it is not totally alien. In the cell it is discovered, so many more times than not, that the grace of God is available to very ordinary people in the process of being themselves and suffering through their alienation. They are people who no longer feel their place in traditional Swedish society or the physical space necessary for new social and religious realities, and who help form the core of a vast movement of migration to North America. They are people learning to gather in little circles, to find themselves a home because they have been deprived of their home. In the midst of the earthquake they are finding the security of the tribe. Uprooted, they have found each other and God has found them, they believe, in the midst of the circle. And very soon they discover what all such wanderers discover, that having been uprooted was not necessarily an act of cruelty or malice, that it was, in fact, an act of liberation.

The evidence that these people had been liberated in their religious experience and uprooting may be found in the hymnody still sung by Covenant people. If you spend an hour reading and then singing the hymns of Oskar Ahnfelt, Lina Sandell, Nils Frykman, and A. L. Skoog, and hear in it anything but a kind of surprised childlike joy at what they had discovered in the midst of the darkness of their alienation and uprooting, then you hear something vastly different than I. Those of us who have worked at translating these Swedish songs of the Pietist heritage, know that they are beautiful and tough-knit lyric celebrations of the personal discovery that even the wanderer on the road in the company of friends has the possibility of God's companionship.

I am fully aware that I speak as a college teacher with a quarter-century of experience at the same place. Some wanderer! Middle-class, with the hope of Social Security coming to me along with a pension, I have spent most of my life teaching middle-class virtues to my kids, which includes not being uprooted, being where you ought to be when you ought to be, playing guitar in church but not on the open road. I can only read the accounts of immigrant kids—six years old, seven years old, ten years old, twelve years old—coming with tags around their necks to Castle Garden in New York. Meanwhile, I recall my twenty-one-year-old son, strong as a moose and healthy as an ox, wanting to go alone to the East Coast, and my response: "Not until I got some proper idea of what you're gonna do there." We have reached the point where we can laugh about that now (at least I have). The record of the immigrant experience shows how fragile a thing human life is, and yet how extraordinarily resilient it can be—how impossible it seemed that anything could survive that earthquake, and yet how remarkably the earthquake *was* survived, and with what beauty. New shoots sprang up in some of the least likely places in the world. After the storm there was a new growth.

Those who lived through it, however, could hardly have appreciated those possibilities. And I am simply offering the observation that this is happening to us right now. In my bones I feel that we are being uprooted now in a variety of ways, personally and communally. We are pulled in all kinds of strange directions, led out, as it were, by fishhooks and captors, in one direction or another, dispersed all over the world. Little wonder that people feel so small and vulnerable to attack, just as were our forebears, who nevertheless found in strange places moments of unutterable anguish and loneliness, suddenly a comforting hand and a voice that says, "You are not alone. I have purposes. I have things to be done." Uprooting is one of the stages, but it is not the only stage. The possibility is therefore real, it seems to me, based on a reading of Scripture and the history of the Church, that the experience of uprooting may be a deliberate act of God to bring us back to a faithfulness to him and to his purposes, from which we have wandered by reason of our self-satisfaction and presumed stability. Our own tradition in the Covenant Church gives us reason to have confidence that people can be thrown bodily out of their accustomed culture and can create new things as a consequence.

CHAPTER 2

Planting

Having addressed the pilgrim experience as one of first being driven out of a relatively secure world, this chapter takes up the theme of planting in a more or less chronological fashion. While planting is also a part of the later stages of fencing and managing, we are especially concerned here with the experience of a first planting, what one does out of necessity following the period of exodus and wandering. The pilgrim, having been driven out, is also driven to plant.

Those who have been uprooted—in the Old and New Testaments, as well as in subsequent history—are wanderers like our primitive human ancestors. These are the hunters and gatherers, living like the children of Israel on manna and quail gathered daily, and grumbling because they could not make it last an extra day. Or they depended on their livestock, like Abraham and his crew, perpetually searching for enough pasturage to feed the animals and thus to get wool and mutton for themselves. For the uprooted, life means moving constantly, using the earth as a kind of vast "warm storage freezer" (as one of my colleagues put it). They gather where there is gathering to be done and hunt where there is hunting to be done, live gratefully with the earth and always see new things. The problem with that kind of life is that there cannot be many such people. And those who live by hunting and gathering always live in small groups. The best anthropological evidence we have indicates that the size of the primary group cannot exceed more than thirty people. The whole tribe, the face-to-face tribe, probably cannot be more than five hundred. The reason for this, of course, is that the carrying capacity of the land will not sustain any more than this. And that way of life, therefore, is always a way of life at the expense of children. Or, if not at the expense of children, then at the expense of the old, who can no longer maintain the line of march and have to be left behind to die.

Consider Abraham. His covenant with Yahweh really meant, did it not, giving up his own accustomed way of life. I do not mean principally his life in Ur of the Chaldees or in Haran, but rather his identity as a Bedouin sheik, the master of his whole clan and of his flocks. This included his freedom to move in and out of the more settled areas of Palestine pretty much as he pleased, making his treaties and serving his own interests. In that fateful moment when the angel of the Lord came to Abraham and said, "Your wife, Sarah, is going to conceive," and when Sarah stood back in the tent and laughed, the naming of the child Isaac became a marvelous commentary on the wholeness of those ancient patriarchs. For us, of course, that word conjures up all sorts of reverenced certainties, but *Isaac* simply means "he laughed." I like that. I like that direct way of remembering an argument between Abraham and God, the feeling of the improbable. But when the promise comes to Abraham that "your descendants shall be as the sands of the seas," that means inevitably, in the whole world in which we live, that Abraham had to stop wandering. Somewhere down the line, his descendants had to become farmers. There is no other way to become the most numerous progeny on earth except to farm. That is the way of the world.

Therefore, when Abraham spared Isaac on Mount Moriah, he committed his progeny and his covenant with God to a life of planting. He not only did that, he also altered his sense of the divine, which he had inherited from his old Chaldean ancestors. In Ur of the Chaldees, and in Mesopotamian culture in general, there was through many generations a grisly habit: the father always secured the safety of his house, just as the king always secured the safety of his city, by burying his firstborn in the cornerstone of the building. When, therefore, Abraham spared Isaac, the true test was not that he was willing to bring Isaac to the altar; the true test was that he was willing to let Isaac live. It meant in this double sense that he had to believe God for his security as he committed his progeny to a life of farming, which is like changing one's life from the freedom of the open air to all the necessary commitments and long-term ambiguities of the settled life.

I take that as a kind of allegory about our human situation. The anthropologists are now saying that people did not spring quickly and gladly to farming. They did not leave their life of gathering and hunting joyfully. And this solves a problem that has puzzled contemporary anthropologists, who have gone out and seen tribes that live by hunting and gathering and have no more than a two- or three-day work week. How does that grab you? Of course, they do not have automobiles, televisions, computers, and all the other things that we associate with progress. But what they do have is an enormous amount of time to enjoy each other, because they live in a world that in their own environment is balanced. And now the anthropologists are suggesting that no sensible primitive people wants to give up their existing way of life or the tribe, because it is their essential life context. If one is in balance, one is at ease and life is good. People are driven to farming, however. And the theory now is that along the great river-based civilizations— the Nile, the Tigris-Euphrates, the Yellow River of China—some hunters and gatherers discovered the enormous richness of the riverine world. With plenty of wild fowl, dependable cereal grasses, and extended growing seasons, settlements flourished as the carrying capacity of the land sustained larger numbers of people. In time, the population could get so large that some got pushed off into the foothills of the back-country. Survival meant bending the back to the plow and beginning to plant— farming and all that goes with it, which eventually meant what we call "civilization."

So my first point, one that I am using deliberately as a kind of allegory for what our forebears did (be it in Israel, the early Church, or the immigrant experience), is that planting is at its inception not a voluntary but a *driven* activity. We are driven to it out of some kind of obedience, out of some kind of awareness that without planting we die. We accept its implications even though we would have preferred the free life. The uprooted person had experienced the ambiguous mercies of the open road, its joyful lack of responsibility, and the reality that one owed nothing to the earth but only took from it gratefully for daily sustenance, counting on God for the future. That same person is now converted into the anxious husbandman, the worrier, the one who is by the action of planting driven to commitment. Thus the children of Israel came out of the wilderness to all of the difficulties and hazards of the attack upon those fortified cities of the Philistines and of the tribes of eastern Palestine, when there were too many of them to continue to live in the desert. They did it for their children. And if, after all this time, it is possible for us to forget the dangers inherent in that attack, it is because we have not sufficiently imagined the situation in which they found themselves.

When you plant, you commit yourself to stay at least long enough to harvest the crop. Otherwise there is no point in it. Unless, of course, you are Johnny Appleseed, and you just wander around the country eating parts of apples and shoveling the core under the soil so that there will be apple trees all over the landscape. A good many of our Covenant pioneers, it must be noted, were just like Johnny Appleseed, traveling around the country digging down apple cores with a joyful kind of abandon, never intending to come back, or only casually, but confident that if they put a seed there, there would be a tree sooner or later. For most of us, however, the necessity is to stay there, at least until the harvest. And that means that you commit yourself to being in the neighborhood, even though you are by the very act of planting committing a major act of faith in a whole lot of ways. When you begin to plant, you have to wait on life. You have to wait on life that you cannot even see. Put a piece of seed in your hand, any kind of seed. I take a little seed, just a dot, barely visible, and only then through the bifocals now. And I ask myself, what do I see in that seed that looks anything like a flower? Nothing. I get it out of a package that says "Marigolds." To help my unbelief they put a picture of the marigold on the package. But I assure you that when I put that seed in the ground, it has no relationship to the marigold at all. It is only the memory of some kind of connection between the seed and the mature plant that justifies so silly a thing as putting into the ground a little speck, that may or may not contain within it all the mysteries of life. And I hold on to this memory for dear life. I cannot see it, nor can I demonstrate it. And if I try, I will kill the seed. I can boil it, cut it open, put it in the ground and every day I can pick it up to see what is happening to it. Is this not how we often behave about the seed we plant in the church? We are always grubbing around at the roots. "Hey! How are things going? Hey, if we pull it up and have a look at it, we can tell if it is really growing!"

I put the seed in the ground. It is an act of faith. I agree to stay there until the growing season has brought, by the mercy of God, the plant to maturity. And then everything is at the mercy of the environment. Remember the parable of the sower? The seed falls on stony ground. The birds come, the corn borers, the root eaters. The world is full of predators. It does not rain. It rains too much. It rains at the wrong time. City people are accustomed to identifying farmers almost immediately by their consciousness of rain. They always seem to complain: "Yes, it's a nice rain, but there wasn't enough." "It should have come yesterday." "Why couldn't it wait four days?" And so on. That is the way with people who are utterly dependent upon an environment they cannot control. Both the seed, which they cannot create, and the environment, which they cannot control, are indispensable to the final growth of the mature plant. The only role of the planter is the willingness not to eat the seed, but to put it in the ground, with the willingness to stay there and do what little one can in the company of the seed (maybe to talk to it) until the plant is mature. Everything is given; nothing, or very little, in the process can be controlled.

Those who have committed themselves to planting have therefore pledged themselves to a major act of faith, the future of which cannot really be certain. In fact, the odds may more often than not be poor, especially because the planter is driven to this activity by one's poverty and is almost always in debt. There is no other way to work the mechanism. If one had the capital to pay for the venture, then the planter is in reality a manager. If one could control the process, then the planter becomes a manufacturer. If one could control the environment, then the farmer becomes the expert of agribusiness. In short, one then succeeds in having taken some of the uncertainty out of it. One can proceed less in faith, with less vulnerability. And, of course, there is in each of us a desire to do precisely that. One of the things about being responsible human beings is that we want to reduce uncertainties, we want to reduce the area of variability; we want if possible to exert maximum control over the process.

There is something mysterious, both in the life of the church and in the life of the seed, that resists submission to that kind of manipulation. Tampering results in hybrids, which are very nice for consumption but which are also sterile and cannot be used for subsequent seeding. Perhaps a consequence of our recent "green revolution" is that we have now succeeded in standardizing our hybrid seed processes to the point where we are dependent on relatively few cereal grains. The easing of population pressures in relation to food may become subject to new interventions by predators since the whole enterprise rests on a handful of varieties, thus leaving us more vulnerable than before. Which is to say that, for the planter, not controlling the process is to accept a certain kind of freedom not to be responsible for tinkering around with things that are not understood and may have unforseen consequences when it comes to feeding the human race. We shall leave this argument to the experts, and I am not asking you to accept it, just to think about it, because hybridization always involves some God-like activity for which we may not in the long run be very well equipped. Once again we have to rely on God's sense of humor and his ability to create diversities that we do not understand and that sometimes are inconvenient for us, but that in the long run are good for us as children.

Well then, back to the seed. We cannot make it. We only save it after an earlier harvest—either our own or someone else's. I offer a story in this respect. It is familiar, because it is part of the American oral tradition. It illustrates one of the puzzling things about the first days of European settlement in America—and it made no difference whether it was the English, Spaniards, French, or Scandinavians. When they first came to America they brought their seed with them, their European seeds, the ones that they were accustomed to, the ones they knew about. What else would they bring? But they speedily discovered that those seeds did not do well in the American environment, at least not at first, where they had no choice but to survive.

Imagine, for instance, that area inside Cape Cod that we today call Plymouth. In the first place, those pilgrims arrived there in November, which is not a great time for planting. Those of you who have had the experience of a November on the New England coast have some notion of what the hope was that they *could* survive. In the second place, none of them were farmers. They were all city people, small craftsmen, lower- to middle-class people, who knew little about farming. And they had with them European cereal grains—wheat, oat, barley, rye—that required cleared fields. Now, if there is something that New England lacked in 1620, it was cleared fields. What they had were endless forests, second growth, and bramble. The only thing even resembling a cleared field was what the Native Americans, who had been devastated by a smallpox plague in that region, had cleared in order to plant their corn. But they never had been senseless about energy. They did not clearcut the trees, creating broad, flat fields. They just girdled the trees to keep them from growing leaves, and they planted the corn in the middle in nice little hills that required sunshine but not the moldboard plow, which they lacked anyway. So that when these cultured, civilized Europeans tried to plant their wheat, they discovered that they had years of work ahead of them rooting out the tangled bramble.

This is where God's humor comes in again. They are at a loss. They are European. Their eyes are closed to other kinds of seed. They are surrounded on all sides by oceans of fish (the cod fish became, after all, the "sacred cod" of Massachusetts), beaches laden with clams, rivers running with fish, and forests haunted with game. And they were *starving*—because they wanted to eat European; because they were stuck with their own seed. And then one day a native man appeared (called an Indian because of Columbus's error of location, one that has persisted smugly in European ethnocentricity long after it was known to be an error), and inquired in their own English language if he could be of help. His name was Squanto, and he was alone. His village had been wiped out, and he was the only surviving member of the Patuxet tribe. It was the village on the site of which the so-called Pilgrims were now living, the saints of Plymouth. He had been kidnapped by Europeans years before and taken to England, where he learned English. He stowed away on a ship that got him to Newfoundland, and he migrated down the coast and arrived just in time to give these people some exercises in the planting technology appropriate to their new world. Now, if that were written in a novel, would anyone believe it? And what did Squanto tell them? He explained to them, in effect, what they had already learned, much to their despair: their seed would not grow under the circumstances under which they would now have to plant. They discovered that they needed the most important seed of the New World, corn. This is what is meant by the assertion that the same act in a different culture is a different act. The same seed in a different environment may not flourish, at least until the environment has been created in which that seed can adapt itself to the new world.

What then is the seed that we are concerned about here, that is, the seed of the planting generation, of the transplanting generation from Europe to America? In the case of Sweden specifically—and it is only one of several such cases—the seed that was available for planting was a half-century of primary experience in the cell, the small group, and the reflection upon and memory of that experience. These cells, often in the midst of great upheaval and change, were the places where lay people had received a serious biblical education, with its application in daily living. The heart of this movement had been networked and promoted within a significant national magazine, *Pietisten* (The Pietist), which was edited by Carl Olof Rosenius and appeared monthly. Each month the periodical would bring a sermon to the cell, to the conventicle. The sermon came in the magazine; it did not have to come with the preacher. The preachers of the renewal movement were few and far between, largely itinerants, so the sermon came in the magazine, and it came in a way that the writer, particularly Rosenius, understood would be most usable to the people in the cells. The paragraphs were short and they were all numbered, so that usual method in the cell of reading around the circle could be followed simply and efficiently. Each person had a number to read, all the way around. And those who could not read very well were still able to participate, because they knew which number to point to and follow with their peasant, callused fingers. They helped each other around the circle as they read God's word, Luther's catechism and sermons, and sang the old psalms and the newer evangelical songs. These emigrants to a new world not only brought the cell with them, but the accumulated experience of that which had nurtured them in the long years of community.

This biblical and homiletical education took place in a context, however, that it is very difficult for us to appreciate today. It took place in the context of a primary fellowship, which we can recognize was warm, but which was also knowing and realistic. It took place in a social context where people had been living for hundreds of years without interruption, and where there were no secret skeletons in closets. The town gossip knew everything. If you were a tailor in that cell fellowship and the sleeves of the coats you sewed fell off, you would hear about it in the next cell meeting. And somebody was sure to say, "Saint Paul never sewed tents like that!" If you were mean to your children, if you were not paying your bills, if you had a glowing testimony but your life was a bag of worms, you heard about it in the cell, and they said, "Shut up!" They did. There was an unvarnished directness. There is a story from my mother about her father, the immigrant preacher, Ole Myhren, who was a great barge of a Norwegian. He first did his preaching backed up against a bar in a Michigan lumbering town, with the prefatory statement, "I'm going to preach until somebody knocks me down." And he preached a lot. He was a formidable presence, faithful to the last drop of his blood to the process of planting—more planting than harvesting. And when he ran into difficult people in his little congregation in Sacramento or Hilmar, California, and they started to smart off about this or that, not yet dry behind the ears and of a malicious and troublesome temper, he just said, "Sit down, Ernest." And Ernest sat down.

The materials with which the planters worked, and the sense of the seed that they had, came out of that kind of authentic experience. They usually said what they meant, because they had not yet learned, really, that there was value in being gentle. Perhaps there was even a calculated value to be acquired in being devious. Such was the case because for the most part they had not learned the necessity of dealing in a direct sense with others apart from those they knew on a face-to-face basis. They felt secure with them. Besides this primary fellowship, they had learned (and this is, of course, their primary lesson for us, and it is the very kernel of the seed) to trust Jesus as brother and as Lord. To him, as a person, they had a fierce and unshakeable commitment. This suggests the *full life* of the cell, which these people simply inherited, experienced, and then brought with them to the New World.

But this is not enough. They had one other thing. And I have to say that this is maybe the most important thing I have learned. It took me a long time. I did not get it from the literature. It became clear to me when we spent six months in Sweden and were able to experience the Swedish people, which is different than having lived in a Swedish-American context. I spent my whole boyhood in Swedish-speaking services among Swedish Americans. My wife, Barbara, and I were tremendously impressed when we landed in the city of Jönköping in 1976. It seemed to us that almost everybody in Jönköping was a Covenanter. Well, it turned out that everybody in Jönköping was a *Swede*. It is strange what ideas lack clarity until one is there.

The thing I am getting to is this: those cells were organic *cells*, which necessarily means that they were cells within the stabilizing and traditional framework of the Church of Sweden. They were not independent creations. They did not stand alone. And they did not assume any responsibilities outside of the life of their cells that were already being assumed by the Swedish state church. These people were free of all of the work carried out by bishops, priests, and theological schools, knowing that it would be done by others in the customary way. Quite often they criticized it as being badly done, but never did they suggest that it ought not to be done at all. And they were not separatists. They saw themselves, as the Halle Pietists saw themselves, ideally, as a body of Jesus's friends inside the Church. And in this respect they embodied implicitly a powerful critique of many of the practices of the established church. They continued, however, to belong to the Church of Sweden. Even as a matter of choice, since the beginning many Covenanters, though committed to the free, believers' church idea, have retained their membership in the Church of Sweden. This has not been a mere matter of convenience or tax advantages, but a connection that symbolizes that they are not a sectarian or separatist people. My experiences living in Sweden helped me understand aspects of myself, as one connected to the seed that came out of the renewal movement of nineteenth-century Sweden and the migration of Swedes to North America. And some of it had little to do with theology or the fact that I am a Christian. It stands as a kind of case study for the particularity of the roots and history as applied to each of us, whether we want to inherit it or not. It simply comes to me and to you as seed.

The seed that was going to be planted in North America, therefore, was this long, long memory of the growth of an authentic biblical, spiritual experience in a cell form, which had as its indispensable context this kind of society and this kind of church. It was the only seed they had with them on their journey to the new land. And they tried to plant that seed exactly as they had planted it in Sweden. In Chicago, for example, a relatively large group of recently arrived immigrants from Jönköping, many of whom had been members of the Jönköping Mission Society (the very Jerusalem of the *läsare*, those known as "readers"), went looking for the closest thing they could find to the Church of Sweden. This was the great Immanuel congregation, presided over by Erland Carlsson, and a member of the Augustana Synod. And what did they do? They met Erland Carlsson, who was also a follower of Carl Olof Rosenius, the revival leader in Sweden, and said, "We want to start a mission society inside this congregation." Carlsson understood them and said, "Fine." But the Lutheran members of the congregation, who had been there a little bit longer and were a little more sensitive, said, "You're making a terrible mistake. This is no longer Sweden and this is not the Church of Sweden. In America, we don't have a state church. If you want to have a church, you go out there and build your own church."

These people had been brought up as Swedes to believe that to leave the church meant to lose one's vote, if not one's soul. One could not even leave it by dying. But during revival times in Sweden, leaving the church meant becoming a Baptist or a Methodist—sectarians. Few were willing to go to that depth of humiliation, because it meant that you had declared yourself at war with the society. They came to America only to discover that they no longer were in a recognizable context. They were told, "The whole world out here is free." This came with a price, however. On the vast plains of America, the Norwegian immigrant Per Hansa, in Ole Rølvaag's *Giants in the Earth*, thought, "This is a free world. It goes from horizon to horizon." But his wife, Beret, kept looking for the boundary stakes. She kept looking for the limits, and there were no limits. And she went mad.

On the high plains of America—in this vast, raw, uncultivated land, in this rich, inexpressibly huge land, where you could get 160 acres *free* just for cultivating it, and where the acreage stretched to the setting sun without any sign of a limit—there was also nothing to break the wind. There was nothing to stop the hurricane. There was no Gulf Stream to moderate the temperature. One went from a freezing blast to a Chinook wind overnight. And just as in the geographical world, so in the spiritual world. America could be a madhouse of bitterly competing religious sects, and Swedish Americans soon learned how to join in the competition among themselves. With all of this planting, often by unbridled itinerant proselytizers, and an insufficient attention to fencing, the religious landscape was often confusing. A few examples will suffice.

Among early Swedish Lutherans in America, there were many competing voices before and after the formation of the Augustana Synod in 1848. In 1845, Peter Kassel led a group of immigrants to a colony he called New Sweden, located about forty miles west of Burlington, Iowa. The first years were lean and hard despite the rich soil. Many died of disease and exposure. But in time the colony expanded, and when it came time to organize a church in 1848, because of a lack of trained and credentialed clergy the colony turned to a young cobbler, Magnus F. Håkanson. He tried his best to hold the flock together as one by one the competing proselytizers came through the area. Frankly, the young, green, and uneducated Håkanson was little match for their zeal. First came Gustaf Unonius from Chicago with his Episcopalian pressures. Then it was Jonas Hedström and his fiery brand of Methodism. To this, many members of the colony and Håkanson himself succumbed. Finally the Baptists came in the persons of Gustaf Palmquist and F. O. Nilsson. Many were rebaptized. Even Håkanson had made such plans, but demurred after several of the leading lay Lutherans in the community helped him recover his equanimity. No wonder people could be so vulnerable on the prairie, or anywhere else for that matter, when their own spiritual leaders were not rooted in their planting, much less prepared for the task. But that is the point: few of them were. In terms of Covenant history, this same Håkanson would become the pastor of the little Lutheran church in Swede Bend, Iowa, where revival broke out in the middle 1860s, and where another cobbler, Carl August Björk, would emerge as the leader of the Mission Friends, and ultimately the Covenant's first president.

Sometimes the efforts at planting in the early days occurred in places where the soil was unstable. A Swedish Lutheran congregation with twenty-five to thirty members had been formed in May 1857 in a rural settlement known as Cannon River, a few miles from the village of Cannon Falls, Minnesota. Eric Norelius, a recent seminary graduate living in nearby Vasa and who helped organize many early congregations, came by to help the congregation plan for a building. Pledges were secured and a foundation laid. Norelius walked seventeen miles to Hastings, ordered the lumber and had it hauled. Most of the families, though, were given to land speculation, and before the walls were even erected most had taken off for a nearby county. The pile of lumber disappeared as locals (including some from the church) simply helped themselves; Norelius was forced to secure a loan at 4 percent interest, which he faithfully paid off over time. Only one person had sufficient conscience to give him a sack of flour in compensation for the building materials he had stolen.

In the midst of competing groups planting in the same places and at the same times, confusion and potential violence often reigned. Charles Anderson, a Dane who, throughout the 1870s selflessly aided the Swedish Mission Friends—those who would in time become Covenanters—reported in his newspaper about efforts he participated in to plant a church in Bucklin, Missouri. The initial meeting spawned conflict, as others stormed the meeting with axes and planks in hand, yelling for the intruders to leave—or else. Many in the hostile crowd were staid members of the frontier community, and feared that these new proselytizers were "free-thinkers." Now, if there was ever a man who was not a free-thinker, it was Charles Anderson. He was a very orthodox, evangelical Lutheran. But he had gotten identified with the wave of new planters who had come in, and those who had planted before were not going to have them there. They were doing something that will be addressed specifically in the next chapter: they were fencing. They were establishing boundaries. And thus what the planters discovered was that it could be dangerous, that you might pick acreage that had already been marked out by others who were also in the process of planting. And it was for these people—who were basically a shy, not terribly assertive or excitable, and certainly not terribly rights-conscious people—like coming into a cold bath after a warm sauna. You felt so alone. You felt so unarmed. You felt so undefined.

In addition to this, these sowers, who went from place to place looking for their immigrant compatriots in order to preach the word to them, were universally poor. They had very little, and some of them absolutely nothing. It remains somewhat of a mystery how they could do it year after year in that kind of poverty. They had their black valise, they wrote like beggars to the railroads for ministers' passes, and they slept on people's floors overnight, glad for shelter but certainly receiving little else. It certainly helped that most were young, but at the same time many had growing families, and they were gone from home much of the year.

It is a simple fact that there would not have been a Covenant Church at all except that they planted, because the vast majority of Swedes wanted nothing to do with them. As best we know, the Augustana Synod and the Covenant, as well as the other Swedish-American churches (Methodist, Baptist, Episcopalian, and Free), together never made up much more than 20 percent of the total Swedish migration. It is not fair for us to declare that the others were lost, but we may conclude that they wanted nothing to do with those pre-migration memories. And the vast majority of them wanted nothing to do with churches. Those plantings had to be made in the teeth of the opposition of the people. The struggle to maintain the Church of Christ in any generation is a struggle of sacrifice by those who have accepted the responsibility to plant. And the endless labors of those struggles can never be repaid in this world. We trust they will be repaid in another. Those who plant must call unmindful people to the necessity of providing for children, that is, for the future; of committing where they would rather be free; of labor in behalf of something, the end of which they cannot hope to see. Those who sow are the servants of a vision beyond their imagination. And the resulting plant is organically one, where all sustain each other by the grace of God. In a spiritual, if not physical, sense, the planters—be they clergy or lay—are those who know poverty and who live by faith.

CHAPTER 3

Fencing

Familiar to many people is the line in Robert Frost's famous poem, *Mending Wall*: "Something there is that doesn't love a wall, that wants it down." There is something in the very word *fencing* that sounds ominous. And it may be, of course, that for most of us our perception of fencing is a high-plains sense, that by "fence" we understand barbed wire. Anyone who has tangled with barbed wire, or has been tangled in it, knows what a threatening thing barbed wire can be, how it almost never kills you but it nags you to death—just keeps nipping, jabbing, and tearing, subjecting you to constant and humiliating irritation. I was never tall enough to climb clean over one. I had to climb between, and as often as not my jacket was caught on the top rank and my pants were caught on the bottom one, and while I struggled to get one loose, the other tore.

The walls of New England, however, are of another kind. They look lovely; they are picturesque. These fences are a reminder of good order in the cultivated countryside, a reminder that people have lived there for a long time and that the land is no longer raw. I think our feeling about it would be somewhat different if we ever had had to make a stone fence in New England, because all those stones came out of the fields. And the reason for the fence is, among other things, that there was no other good place to put the stone, so they made a wall of it. The stones keep working their way up following each winter; the memory of the ancient glaciation is there along the countryside as you drive over those picturesque roads. Perhaps the split rails of our eastern woodland tradition, associated with Abraham Lincoln's frontier, are equally picturesque. Durable, blending nicely into nature in their zigzag pattern, they meander across the countryside. They are never straight, you know, and it is a lovely thing. They sort of wind around, following the terrain and looking, therefore, less inhuman.

The problem with barbed wire is that it is our own invention, as the consequence of rational application of thought to a terrible problem. Time and time again you find the early Swedish planters declaring with amazement that all of the trees that are now to be found, say by 1890, on their property or around their churches were planted by themselves when there was not a tree in sight. And for years Swedes and others stayed away from the high plains, calling it the "great American desert," on the quite mistaken grounds that if the land could not support trees, it certainly could not support anything else. They were absolutely wrong. The land was so rich that trees never stood much of a chance. The merest little prairie weeds would crowd out the tree seedlings. And once people discovered the richness of those plains, it became necessary for them to find a means of protecting the planting.

That, of course, is what fences are all about—to protect the planting. To ship in wood from across the Mississippi River was prohibitively expensive. To try and find in that deep prairie soil any stone at all was impossible, unless out on the margins of the high plains. It was necessary then to have some kind of fence that could cover those enormous distances without creating a great weight problem or without making it so expensive that nobody could afford to use it at all. And the answer to it was barbed wire. String two strands of wire together and put a little cut knob in between them in a way so that it could not slip out easily, and heavy animals and other creatures are persuaded that it would be less than wise to attack the fence. Without the barb, you know, there is nothing in that wire to discourage even the dreamiest cow. And this invention suddenly swept across not only the plains of America, but the world as well.

I have to say that I think barbed wire is intrinsically ugly. It looks awful and is a nasty sort of sign. But despite its nastiness, it is a sign in what was essentially a beneficent errand, that is, to protect the planting. If you had gone out on the high plains and planted corn or wheat and suddenly found yourself in the middle of an invasion of bison, half-a-million of them in the course of a day, there was nothing left of the planting. On a landscape of such vast and seemingly illimitable horizons, if you wished to protect your stock, the only solution was to build a good fence, because fences not only fence out, they also fence in. So there was nothing to do but to accept barbed wire and try to forget that it could also be used on the Western Front to declare "no man's land" and to impale men in the bright glare of the phosphor shells.

I am assuming that the primary job of fencing is to protect the planting, and that, in the church as in our general society, to fence is fundamentally to protect the planting, although there are other reasons. Fences also declare property. They say what is yours as against what is somebody else's. This is perhaps the most ancient activity of social humanity: to declare what is his or hers. Some of the most interesting implied fences in human history are those four stone posts, which the ancient Romans worshiped. They put them at each corner of their property, and they called them "the terminal gods." Once that stone was planted, it was an act of blasphemy to touch it, much less to move it. It defined the boundaries of the Roman family, for whom the god was always the ancestor and whose spirit was alive in the hearth. In that patriarchal society, it was Grandfather burning in the hearth, and the eldest living male was high priest; it was an altar not to be approached by any stranger. The gods of the hearth (the Penates of the lintel, which guarded against impious eyes seeing the secret worship of the family; and the Lar, the gods of the fire, for which the appropriate wood had to be kept all year), along with the gods of the terminal boundaries, secured the exclusivity of the Roman family and its religion—a space into which no stranger could be brought. It was a religion of his family and of his family alone; and all his future welfare depended upon the skill with which he propitiated the ancestors' graces.

For instance, the risk of hernia that so many men have undergone trying to take their brides across the threshold, is the direct consequence of a Roman custom dictating that a woman brought into a new family from another family would be in mortal danger from the impiety of observing the strange hearth; she had, therefore, to be brought in under the guise of kidnapping. It was a kind of religious kidnap: you brought her in by force so that the fault could not be laid to her. And the first ceremony through which she went prior to her marriage was the disfranchisement from her father's house and the enfranchisement in her husband's house. She had, in short, to become alien to her family and to become instead family to a new god. The fences between those Roman families sooner or later had to be combined in some way to make Roman society possible in its disciplined and world-conquering way.

Thus fences can define the boundaries of our responsibility to each other, and the boundaries of our resources vis-à-vis other people. Fences also limit and control access to our property: where we put the gates, who has a right to open or lock them, and what kind of signs go on them. What is the door into the sheepfold? It is only the existence of the fence that makes the existence of the door possible. And the one who has a right to enter it and to be known by the sheep, to be recognized as the shepherd, is thus defined functionally, in a sense, by the existence of that fence for the protection of the sheep. The point is that when you fence something, you announce the existence and define the nature of settlement. We are no longer uprooted. We are no longer merely planting. We have decided to stay. This is the way we are staying. And this is the way we see ourselves as we stay. Something is always inside the fence, and something is always outside the fence. In our own experience, we always put up fences when we fear attack or if we want to keep something out or else keep something in. As Robert Frost said later in his poem: "Before I built a wall I'd ask to know/What I was walling in or walling out,/And to whom I was like to give offense."

The other thing, of course, is that the minute you put up a fence, you are committing yourself to mending it. The things just do not stay up. They are constantly eroding, or someone is always driving through them, or something is always burrowing under them. And you must walk the fence and see whether the boundaries are appropriate. Whether or not the surveyor has been there, the fence is there, and it makes the implicit explicit; and therefore once it *is* there, it must be physically protected. The fence itself sometimes becomes the preoccupation of the fencer rather than the thing that the fence was originally made to do. I want to keep that distinction before you, please, because I think it is important for our subsequent discussion: the fence itself can become the preoccupation rather than the function for which the fence was originally made, simply because the fence wants to fall down.

This metaphor is admittedly imprecise, but at least it gives us a starting point toward understanding the possibility of a further stage in the development of the pilgrim experience. Whether you understand my metaphor theologically or sociologically, or (as I hope) both, makes no real difference. Yet, I want to argue that it is sometimes impossible to understand the life of a group in any realistic sense unless you simultaneously understand both its theology and its sociology, and see how they link with each other.

Let us reflect for a moment on the history of the people of Israel when they are defining themselves, which is to say, fencing. They are doing it every time they celebrate Passover, and also in their reflections on those ceremonies, which come after the event. "Why is this night like no other night in the year? Why are we a people unlike any other people in the world? Because we were brought out of Egypt by the mercy of God, by the angel of the Lord." And because, as Miriam exclaimed triumphantly on the other side of the Red Sea, "The horse and its rider has he thrown into the sea! Behold, the Lord has triumphed gloriously!" That is a fence that structures the inside and the outside of the people Israel. It is not to be understood necessarily negatively or positively. It is, however, an element in the structure by which these people have come to define themselves.

There are many examples of this fence building: when Moses came with the Decalogue and with the associated pentateuchal commands; when the judges made their pronouncements; when Israel received the laws of King David; when she received the prophecies of Isaiah and Jeremiah, Amos and Micah; and when she lived through those enormously harsh and restrictive reforms of Ezra after the captivity, and cooperated with Nehemiah in the rebuilding of the walls. When she suffered the final Diaspora, and continued to live, as she does now, through Torah and midrash, in the ceremonies of the synagogue, and in the memory of the patriarchs. Israel is announcing by her fences who she is and what she believes her destiny to be. She knows how she has been planted and what are the plants that need to be protected.

So it is with the church. We read the gospels, the epistles, the pastoral epistles, the Revelation according to St. John. We read in the whole New Testament and draw from it a set of structures by which we mean, in each time and place, to define ourselves for ourselves and as over against others. There are inescapably people *in* it; there are inescapably people *out* of it. There is no other way to say it. When we read the councils of the early church, the three-hundred-year struggle to define the Trinity, to declare in mere human words the inexhaustible mysteries of the relationship of the Father, the Son, and the Holy Spirit, we are watching the erection of a fence. When we read the great thinkers of the early church and the medieval scholastics; when we listen to Luther and follow the complex Reformation debates; when we take part in our own imagination in the post-Reformation battles for rule and for survival—in all of this we are watching the construction of systems and structures by which we define ourselves for ourselves and for others.

Perhaps the word *fence* is too limited a word to describe the magnificence of this experience, but it is a word that nevertheless helps us to understand a part of the process through which the pilgrim has to go. It is always a challenge with first-year college students to help them understand that just because an anthropologist speaks of the relative nature of experience—that these people have this custom but that these other people have a different custom—it does not necessarily follow that there is no custom at all. The narrow norms of their own experience having been challenged, students are initially inclined to throw the baby out with the bath. The next task is to get them to recognize that there is no such thing as social humanity without a structure, any more than there is a person standing without bones. That is, the structure is necessarily given. How it is defined and articulated is the problem that each living generation faces, and our pioneers and their succeeding generations were no different than others. Let me rehearse some of them with you.

From John Wesley the line into Sweden went, as you may know, through George Scott, who was brought to Sweden to preach to English workers. They came to help establish industry and new trades in Sweden. Please note that George Scott was in Sweden to preach to the English workers employed by Samuel Owens who were establishing machine shops, as well as to English-speaking commercial leaders and government officials based in Stockholm. He quickly learned Swedish and began to preach to Swedes and not merely to his own people. In short, English Methodism came with the steam engine to Sweden. I like the combination of those two metaphors, because I think Methodism and the steam engine have something to do with each other. And I do not mean it as a criticism. I am speaking of its enormous energy, of its driving force, of its willingness to live inside current technology, and so on. It is to Scott that a sensitive young Norlänning Swede, Carl Olof Rosenius, went to inquire into the state of his soul and to be persuaded that he was, in fact, already saved. From 1842 until his death in 1868, Rosenius became the guiding spirit of the cell movement and the editor of *Pietisten*, the magazine that Scott had begun just prior finally to being driven from Sweden by the hostility of the establishment in Stockholm.

These were not, of course, the only experiences, the only resources from which the new sense of destiny emerged. They came from Spener, the father of Halle Pietism, which was a source of renewal in the German church, finding balance between head and heart. They came as well from Zinzendorf, that strange German count who had established at Herrnhut the ideal society of the brethren (now the Moravian Church), in which there was so much lyricism and so much unaccustomed joy in the good news of the gospel. All of these had influenced not only Rosenius but also Wesley himself, whose own conversion was deeply dependent upon a German set of insights about the possibility of receiving good news with a kind of freedom.

The line from Rosenius, so far as we are concerned, extends forward to Paul Peter Waldenström, who in 1868, when Rosenius died, was a thirty-year-old scholar-pastor, and who was given the editorship of that most significant newspaper, *Pietisten*. Four years later he used that editorship to print a sermon for the twentieth Sunday after Trinity in which he attacked one of the key points of Rosenian, low-church theology. This was a view of the atonement that stated that because of Christ's death on the cross, God's wrath was appeased such that his love toward sinners was once again liberated, establishing the condition for human salvation. If Christ had not died, it was argued, God would have found it impossible, in view of his uncompromising justice, to have shown us grace at all. Waldenström said that that was not a biblical view and set out to demonstrate why. God was, and God is, and God always will be *love*. Jesus did not die to change God's mind; he died to change our minds. Jesus did not die in order to satisfy God's justice; Jesus died in order to make it possible for us to believe in God's love. Jesus became fully human as *God's* act of love to us. And in that lovely, sunny, far from satisfactory but nevertheless optimistic solution of an ancient preoccupation of the church, Waldenström announced an age of acceptance for common humanity. Jesus is your friend. Jesus represents God, who is not the supreme and angry judge, but the supreme and beneficent lover, who calls us constantly to be with him. And this became the good news to thousands of Swedes who were tired of judges and norms that seemed to them irrelevant, and tired of fences that they confessed they could not get across. It seemed like the knocking down of fences. Suddenly, all over Sweden, there was a wild theological dispute. And not only all over Sweden, but in America as well. The dispute centered, of course, on the meaning of the atonement. This is not to say that

Waldenström was completely right about this question. There are difficulties with the view. But it ceased to be simply a question about the nature of God, and became also a question centered on the authority of our understanding about God.

When the atonement debate began, the low-church Lutherans had centered themselves around Rosenius—and that included the people in the National Evangelical Foundation, the chief agency through which good evangelical books had been spread since 1856, and it included most of the Augustana Synod folk here in America. And that is significant. These people saw Waldenström as an enemy who was trying to destroy the Rosenian inheritance. When they saw the colporteurs—those whimsical and sparsely educated planters who rushed around the countryside—they saw disorder and felt the chaos rising like a flood about them, and they were moved immediately to *fence tightly*. Augustana erected a fence in 1875 known as the Galesburg Rule, which was especially designed to curb the Waldenströmian problem: "Lutheran pulpits for Lutheran pastors only. Lutheran altars for Lutheran communicants only." Period. Now, one cannot get a fence much tighter than that. Assuming that you mean by "Lutheran" someone who is willing to subscribe on the dotted line to the unaltered Augsburg Confession, and assuming that the fellowship is easily able to identify these people, then you have sealed the door against chaos. The thief has been prevented from entering. The robber cannot get into the sheepfold. Or, to change the simile, you have battened down the hatches. Let the hurricane come, the old ship will ride it out.

Yet is that the truth of the matter? Or have you just padlocked the door in order to avoid having to consider the problem? So when the Lutherans battened down and said, "Well, that is not Lutheran doctrine. Lutheran doctrine is thus and so," Waldenström announced, "From now on, we will not debate this question according to whether or not it is *Lutheran* doctrine; we will debate it only according to whether or not it is *New Testament* doctrine." And the battle cry became *"Var står det skrivet?"* ("Where is it written?") Just as Pope Leo had feared it would be during the time of Martin Luther, and just as the archbishop of Sweden had feared it would be, the Bible became an instrument of argumentation when in the hands of the layperson. All were free to ponder and decide together the teaching of Scripture in relation to the formulation of doctrine.

As this battle raged in Sweden and America, perhaps it was focused most vociferously among the immigrants in Lindsborg, Kansas. A settlement of the late 1860s, in the early days people gathered buffalo bones off the prairies be ground for fertilizer; the grasshoppers and the hail and the drought regularly frustrated the hopes of the planters; and people lived in sod huts. And they now brandished their Bibles at each other across Main Street in Lindsborg, that muddy track, and said, "You are a Waldenströmian! I won't live with you!" Lindsborg still remembers the atonement controversy. One person in fifty in Lindsborg may know anything specific about the controversy, but most remember that there was a big fight about it. That was fencing.

And what was at stake in the fencing? Well, something of overwhelming importance for Covenanters. In the first place, there is the nature of the final authority of Scripture, a matter that we have far from solved, and which has sometimes been approached with explosive words that can threaten to divide one from another, but of whose importance we cannot possibly have any doubt. That the New Testament is ultimately decisive for our order, fellowship, and discipline, no one in our tradition can dispute. The dispute now centers on in what way is it decisive, and how is it to be specifically understood, and what are the general working rules by which we approach it. And any informed person in the Covenant listens to the possible approach of that debate with some fear and dread, because we have learned from the past that almost inevitably people start losing their tempers very early in the process. Eyes grow red with anger, hair stands on end, and we soon long for a day when people were less theologically sophisticated.

But besides this—besides the principle of the authority of the Bible, which none of the people in those fifty years of cell experience really wanted to contradict at all—there came something else. That is, in the course of the argument with Lutheranism (and these people were, as will be seen in a moment, decisively Lutheran in cast and in tone), the Lutherans made a fundamental mistake. They said, "Unless you accept the Anselmic view of the atonement, you are not really Lutheran." I fail to understand why they did that. Anselm was not a Lutheran. And there was no particular reason to support the notion that this view was particularly dear to Martin Luther, who came four-and-a-half centuries after Anselm. Scholarship has demonstrated that. Something else was at stake here. This was an argument about one thing that was really in the settlement of something else. And nobody at the time was entirely clear *what* it was about.

But when the Mission Friends, as they now began to call themselves, responded to this Lutheran assertion, the response was to say, "Well, if we can't believe in the Waldenströmian formulation of the atonement and be Lutherans, then we shall not be Lutherans." This was not the answer the Lutherans wanted. A crucial test involved the admission of candidates to the Mission Institute at Johannelund, a training school run by the Evangelical National Foundation (a Rosenian institution). Waldenström, a provincial delegate of the ENF, soon made it quite clear that he thought that the only test to be applied was not the question, "Do you subscribe to the unaltered Augsburg Confession?" Rather, it was "Do you acknowledge Jesus Christ to be your Savior and Lord?" In short, was there to be a creedal test, or was the test to be a statement of faith in Jesus? For Waldenström, it could only be the latter. For the low-church Lutherans, it could only be the former. The Augustana Synod in America agreed, for this is what it meant to be Lutheran.

For the Mission Friends in America, it meant becoming, as they had in Sweden, increasingly non-creedal. Or to say—as David Nyvall finally, in his clearest way, formulated it—that creeds are all right as local and temporary expressions of what we think. They are the stuff out of which we define things to suit ourselves at any particular time and place. But the inexhaustible source, from which all creeds come, is the New Testament. And in adopting the New Testament, we have potentially adopted all the correct creeds that can ever be formed. For the severe logician or committed creedalist, that leaves something to be desired. It is a meandering fence, unless you have some working rules and some common understandings. But it is a statement about openness. It is a statement that the fence is not going to have a padlocked or unnecessarily narrow gate. It is a statement that the purpose is not to protect the fence, but that the purpose is to protect the planting.

The other great struggle of the same period of time was the struggle around church practice. What is the nature of the church? It focused in the issue of communion, the Lord's Table. If you take communion in the company of manifestly ungodly people (I use their phrase), is that not to violate St. Paul's injunction against taking the communion lightly and therefore to damnation? Since all Swedes were required to take communion once a year (in order to protect their voting rights), and since everyone born in Sweden was a member of the church (regardless of personal decision or inclination), that meant that at least once a year there would be people at the table who did not relate to the communion at all, and who were therefore eating and drinking to damnation. It was repugnant to serious Christians to be associated with these people at the sacred table. They tried to solve that problem by getting away from it and petitioning for the right to observe separated communion. By 1860, communion societies had been constituted under the ENF, officiated over by priests of the state church who had been specifically charged with that responsibility. One of them was Andreas Fernholm, who went on from that, after two years of serving separated communion, to announce that he was no longer a Lutheran, no longer a priest of the state church. He was now a Baptist. This did not help the future of independent communion societies—not in Sweden.

In the course of the ministers' "free church" meetings between 1875 and 1877, Waldenström, E. J. Ekman, and C. J. Nyvall debated with others who shared interests in these same questions, what the nature of the congregation should be—the regenerate church or the folk church? The discussion focused on the Lord's Table. Waldenström made overtures to the Baptists through Carl G. Lagergren, a very responsible leader. And Lagergren said, "Well, it's about time you were getting out of that Lutheran fold. It's about time you recognized the truth of the matter. It isn't because you subscribe to the Augsburg Confession. It's because you love Jesus and are baptized." And Waldenström said, "That's exactly right. Well, let's agree on that, then, and we can be brothers." "Well," said Lagergren, "no, what we have to agree on is that you have to give up infant baptism." This was something that Waldenström, Ekman (though holding the view of believer baptistm), and Nyvall could not do. They were too Lutheran for that. There was adequate evidence, they believed, that the Bible, the New Testament, supported infant baptism. The Baptists said, "Well, if you don't support proper Christian baptism, you can't come to our table."

The Lutherans had closed their table and the Baptists had closed their table. So Waldenström said, "All right, let's change the formulation. Let's all meet together around this one essential question: Each is welcome to be a member of this church who believes in the Lord Jesus Christ. Drop the business about baptism." Then Lagergren said, "Now you're throwing the baby completely out with the bath. You've gotten rid of Christian baptism. We can't live in that kind of world, so you'll have to go your way and we'll go ours." Nor could these free-church-minded people accept the Methodist dictum about sanctification. So they find themselves in the strangest position in late 1877. They are no longer Lutherans, because they do not subscribe to the unaltered Augsburg Confession. They are not Baptists, because they still insist on the rite of infant baptism for those who believe it to be biblical. They are not Methodists, because they do not go along with a holiness interpretation of sanctification. What are they? It is what they are *not*. They are the hole in the doughnut. They are what is left over when everything else specific has been decided. They do not at this time even really have a name. They have called themselves "free Lutherans." Now, increasingly, somebody—and we do not know who it was—begins to coin a word that has a positive ring to it: they are Mission Friends. They are not the only "mission friends" in the world. But this now has a parochial ring to it, a local ring. It is a kind of a wrapping around the property that has a ring that satisfies them, that they are willing to be identified by. It is not so much a theological sound as it is an active sound. They are *Mission* Friends.

And when finally they decide to put together that Mission Friend understanding in the form of an organization, they are faithful to all of those charters. The Swedish Mission Covenant, as it was finally adopted in the summer of 1878, did not require a creedal assertion; it left its table open to all who accepted the lordship of Jesus; it accepted into membership all who followed him, whether they believed in infant or adult baptism; it did not specify any kind of official doctrinal certification; and it established a president and an executive committee to run the Covenant, supervising the work of the church on an annual basis on the authority of what was to be called an annual meeting. This was, at first, all very loose, very chaotic. No elaborate order—except that the first president of the Swedish Covenant, E. J. Ekman, served uninterruptedly for twenty-five years. It was not very chaotic after all.

The problem was not then that they did not know who they were. The problem was to find a label, to put a title on the fence. They knew perfectly well who they were. They knew each other face to face. Their problem was to state it. And it is our constructive problem today. What in the world is the Covenant? Well, you see, it is this little offshoot of the Lutheran movement, a first cousin to the Augustana Synod, but which really is not Lutheran, and so on and so on. Covenant people can easily be embarrassed by those questions. Especially when they ask, "Well, how many of you are there?" and you say, "Well, about sixty-five thousand." And the typical number-conscious American turns away and says, "Sixty-five thousand. Hardly worth defining." Just a drop of spit in a hot skillet, and that is about it. Not much at all, in a world that deals in mega-millions. Sixty-five thousand—it must be a peculiar little thing indeed, a fly-by-night affair—simply because of the absence of quite clearly defined, easily recognized and rationalized labels. And perhaps precisely because of that, for many the Covenant has been more open to life, more open to local peculiarity and vitality, more open to future possibility, and more open to alterations of the boundaries.

In the United States, the Lutheran Mission Friends who had been following Rosenius and Waldenström had been working since 1868 to unite their new congregations in synods, after the American pattern of Lutheranism. The leading figure in the early negotiations was Charles Anderson, who had immigrated as a child with his parents from Denmark. By 1872 he had helped organize both a synod and a school for these Swedish folk of the revival. But because Anderson was Danish, more liberal and confessional, as well as deeply committed to the rapid assimilation and Americanization of the immigrants, he was held in some suspicion. This led to a new synod being organized in 1873, the Mission Synod, which deliberately excluded Anderson from its leadership. This did not deter him, however. He was an active and entrepreneurial man, and he figured that where you had established one synod you could establish still another, and he bounced back the next year in 1874 to found the Ansgar Synod, having first dissolved the earliest synod, which had a strong pan-Scandinavian orientation. By 1874, then, there were two Swedish synods representing different areas where immigrants had settled, but also displaying some significant differences about questions of theology and the nature of the church, which only the eventual formation of the American Covenant in 1885 would resolve. Still, they were all friends, cooperated in many ways, and people could move with ease back and forth. Consequently, even before the Covenant Church in Sweden became a reality in 1878, Mission Friends in America had been organizing on a national basis.

Now, what was the future of these organizations, and what was going to protect the planting? The struggles over atonement and communion were added to by the terrible hurt suffered by many people in the course of that controversy with the Augustana Synod. And the one who suffered most was John G. Princell, who as a pastor in the Augustana Synod, a faithful spiritual child of Rosenius, and a follower of Waldenström and his novel atonement theory, was put on trial in the Augustana Synod for heresy. He came to the not unreasonable conclusion that if you belong to a synod, you could be tried for heresy. That was his experience. And also having been affected by the views of John Nelson Darby's dispensationalism, he drew the conclusion that the only recourse was to do away with synods. And not only synods, but all formal organizational structures that, in his mind, limited the freedom of the spirit and access to fellowship. In short, he argued that Christians, supported only by the good news and in the fellowship of Jesus as shepherd, should do what they can to eliminate human structures, to do away with fences, to let God himself protect the plants, and to keep the fellowship fluid and loose so as to offer the maximum opportunity for freedom.

In a competitive American religious environment, Princell's preaching produced a radical, sectarian wing within the Mission Friend movement. It was intensely fueled by British and American preoccupations with prophetic theories about the last days, and was quite confident that it had penetrated with precision all the deep mysteries of faith and God's will for the world. Whole new lines of conflict were opened up, with the result that both the Ansgar and the Mission synods soon began to be subjected to what could only be called, from their point of view, piratical raids. Congregation after congregation pulled out of those two infant synods to become independent. There were many self-appointed preachers crisscrossing the landscape. One was a charismatic evangelist named August Davis, who divided congregations wherever he went, including Erik August Skogsbergh's tabernacles in Chicago and Minneapolis. This caused near panic in many places, given the ease with which he persuaded new Christians to pull themselves out of these unbiblical churches, and to choose instead the life of freedom in fellowships of believers that had no membership lists, stated budgets, buildings, or any of the impediments that would eventually harden into papal-like structures.

By the mid-1880s it began to appear that if something were not done very shortly, all of the planting that had been done would go down the drain, would be trampled into the earth, and the acreage that had been thus far so hopefully tended would simply be ruined. Whether they were right or whether they were wrong is a matter about which people may readily disagree. But by 1885 even the most conservative of the Mission Synod people had come to the conclusion that some form of common national organization was necessary in order to protect the planting, in order to express the fellowship. Some structure had to be available to give people relationship to each other over time. And they embraced, word for word, the constitution that had been adopted in Sweden seven years before. These people also knew who they were, did not want to define themselves too closely, did not want to fence too securely, but still wanted boundaries. And in the achievement of the Covenant Church, they fixed the boundaries that would provide enough room to maneuver and, at the same time, enough protection for the plants.

In the process, a good many mortal wounds were taken and given between Christians, in ways that not only violated the natural laws of nations and humanity, but even the laws of common courtesy. Lies were spread, rumors were magnified, reputations were traduced—all in the name of theological clarity, and by all sides. The church has often had a very bad reputation for the kind of temper it has exhibited in the middle of its theological and political quarrels. And where it has had the opportunity, it has been positively bloody. Fortunately, in these fights no heads were lopped off. But it was not because there were not those who would willingly have done so, had they had the sword in their hands. But metaphorically, we often do our executions when we are at our most righteous. God save me from the person with righteous indignation! The sinner I can live with. And God save others from me in my righteous moods. The older I get, the more I recognize that the debts for which a merciful God will have to stretch himself most seriously to forgive are the debts I have accumulated in my virtuous moments. They are the ones that have taken me longest to discover and longest to deal with, precisely because I had identified them as virtue.

But now, then, to return to fencing. Is it not true that the people who came as immigrants had had a long and consistent experience of orthodox Christianity, and is that not still true? And the answer to both is of course, yes. It is precisely so because there was no fundamental disagreement among any of these participants: there was no fundamental disagreement about the basics of Trinitarian understanding, the humanity of Jesus and the divinity of Christ; there was no division of opinion about that. That there was a division of opinion about baptism, which would be important to Baptists but relatively unimportant to others, is undeniable. But that people ought to be baptized was universally affirmed. That there would be an end time was proclaimed by all. That the Lord's Table was of central importance to all true believers was celebrated, even if access to it was a matter of disagreement. Our forebears identified with the fence-building of orthodox belief since apostolic times, while preserving its integrity by insisting that everything pertaining to matters of faith, doctrine, and life be tested by Scripture.

It is important in the church and in our common fellowship in the body of Christ to be as clear as we can with each other about our understandings of God in Christ, the rock on which we place our faith, and of our doctrinal formulations. It is also crucial to remember that the Church has been attempting to do this for two thousand years and has not yet succeeded in finding a formulation that is wholly adequate to express the fundamental mystery to which it points. While it may appear to be intellectually sloppy, it is a matter of wisdom to adopt the position of early Covenanters in their debates about communion, atonement, last things, and so on. Skogsbergh said, "It is not always so important to know everything. It is always tremendously important to preach the gospel. So whether I am free or whether I am bound, I may be either and yet preach the gospel. So let us try and stop being omniscient, and get on with the work of planting." And, I think he would have added, in its appropriate way, of church building, and necessarily of fencing. The thing at all costs we have to avoid is the state of mind and the kind of movement that begins to insist that the Christian life is fundamentally a life of doctrine, that that is what the life is. Most Covenanters have not and will not take that position.

There are also sociological fences in the church. The early Covenant, in a pietistic setting that could often be legalistic, imposed constraints on life that may or may not have been biblical. Many of these social norms came naturally to a revivalist culture, be it card playing, dancing, or sabbath observances; but to the young in particular they at times seemed to be matters of dogma divorced from life. Older Covenanters have many stories about how this was experienced in their lives and social groups. This is not to minimize the seriousness of lifestyle questions, but it is to underscore that there are different kinds of fences and boundary-making endeavors even within a unified movement, and that there had better be an integrity and conversation that is honest about these things. It is not enough merely to say it is scriptural without inviting the question, "Where is it written?" Now, if our fences are constricting lives, particularly of our children, in such a way as to make it impossible for them to have a fundamentally honest and thoroughgoing understanding of the New Testament requirements of Christ-like living, then the plant is going to be harmed, if not destroyed.

When you plant, I take it for granted that you fertilize. You do not douse the plants in a disinfectant like Lysol. Lysol may be very nice in the bathroom, though I doubt it. But on a field where young plants are nourished, everyone would agree—no Lysol. If our ethic is to be essentially in the interests of purity, it then cannot be an ethic essentially in the interests of life. Because life requires manure. If the purpose of Christ's death on the cross and his lordship over us is essentially about purity, then I have read the New Testament wrongly. The purpose of Christ's death on the cross for me was essentially for my abundant life—the growth of the plant. I have nothing against purity. I think it is associated with healthy living. But first of all is *life*. The fence must not be built in such a way as to fence out for the purposes of preserving the purity of what is inside. This only ensures a hothouse fellowship incapable of dealing with life's real issues and pressures, as experienced by real people where they are really living. Then the gospel cannot be a saving word of good news. It need not be that way. The purpose of fencing is the plant. The purpose of the plant is nourishment. The purpose of nourishment is life, abundant life. And it ties the pilgrim to the goodness of God, and therefore to the possibility of participation in the usefulness of the pilgrimage.

CHAPTER 4

Managing

Y
ou have forgotten the monthly conference. Your four o'clock
appointment waits in the ante-room. The uptown bureau
is on the wire again.

Most of your correspondence is still unanswered, these bills have
not been paid, and one of your trusted agents has suddenly
resigned.

And where are this morning's reports? They must be filed at
once, at once.

It is an hour you do not fully understand, a mood you have had
somany times but cannot quite describe.

It is a fantastic situation, repeated so often it is commonplace
and dull.

It is an unlikely plot, a scheme, a conspiracy you helped to begin but do not, any longer, control at all.

When they dig you up, in a thousand years, they will find you
in just this pose,

One hand upon the buzzer, the other reaching for the phone,
eyes fixed upon the calendar, feet firmly on the office rug.

This excerpted poem, "Portrait of a Cog," by Kenneth Fearing, expresses something that is eating away at the consciousness of modern
people—certainly at mine. This is an aching sense that one must try,
against all odds, to hold something together that absolutely refuses to
stay in place. There was a time when almost every time I went out of
town, I would have to ask a self-protective question as I returned and
walked in the front door: "What's broken down this time?" The washer,
the dryer, a pump, a roof has caved in, the basement is flooded, a tire has
come off the car or the thing has blown up, the garage door has fallen
off, the dog has bitten the mailman. There is an endless number of Walter
Mitty kind of disasters to which I have come to feel vulnerable because

of the kind of life that we have elected somehow, all unconsciously, to live.

And it is not merely our personal lives that are marked by this kind of daily tension, but our institutional lives as well. For example, you make arrangements for somebody to pick someone up at a certain time. You then receive an angry telephone call informing you the prearranged ride has failed to appear, so you better get over there right now. Or you get to church on Sunday morning, and just at the middle of the organ introit the main circuit breaker trips, and all you get is a sort of a huffy wheeze from the whole instrument—and there was to be a choir extravaganza this morning. Or the sound system has decided to take on a permanent feedback buzz, and no matter where you tune it, it whistles. Or, as the pastor or teacher, you have forgotten your notes—*and* your Bible.

It is this constant sense of a black cloud over your head and that nobody can remember everything, and that you are bound to forget something, and the whole thing is going down the drain. Civilization is going to collapse unless we do something. The church simply cannot last another month unless we do something. The school will not survive another attack like this. *The Covenant Companion* is heading toward extinction. Someone is going to bomb Covenant Offices in Chicago if we do not correct this. Or the latest figures for the most recent fund drive are disastrous. And so on. Until, that is, there comes a morning when you suddenly wake up and you say to yourself, with some kind of minimal humorous self-recognition, "You know, I'm just too tired to care anymore. If it's going down, let it go! And bring me another cup of coffee." You know the feeling.

This is Kenneth Fearing's question, "How did we get ourselves into this kind of position?" In other words, a position where what we mean to say about ourselves is that we are capable of coping but are pursued daily with the expectation that something is coming up and we cannot really make it after all. There is always something loose and flapping. The important distinction, therefore, in the pilgrim experience that belongs to this concept of managing is, in a sense, one that sets it off from the other three categories. It is more closely aligned to fencing, however, than to uprooting or planting. At the root of the problem of trying to manage is the self-expectation that we can and ought to achieve control. Nobody asks of the uprooted that they be in control. It is understood that they are not. In the middle of the hurricane, who expects anyone to maintain normal routines? If you are a pastor, you are lucky even to hang on to the front door. And if the hurricane is real, there might not even be a worship service.

If you think of yourself as a manager, one who exerts control, and is proud of the smoothness with which that control operates, then you have committed yourself to the permanent warfare against enemies both known and unknown, both imagined and unimagined, that assail you from every side. And they have a way of multiplying like dragon's teeth in the night. The fact is, of course, that our control is only an illusion, as we all discover the moment somebody announces a hurricane warning. And then all of our systems of control vanish from our consciousness as matters of power and consequence, and we all run for the cellar and start to pray, "Dear God, let it go over somebody else's house—or, at least, not over mine till I've gotten to the cellar." That is, in the moments when reality intrudes on us, we understand we are not in control. But in all the other moments we must make the pretense. And the reason, I suppose, we must make the pretense is because it belongs with our self-image in the middle of our high-pressure, go-go kind of can-cope civilization.

Pressure. Can cope. Can do. And immediate results—above all, immediate results. It goes with the concepts that are appropriate, not to agriculture in its traditional sense, but to manufacturing in its modern sense. We manufacture to schedule. We have roofed over the process and shut out the rain. We have forced the worker from his old, casual schedule at his loom, and have prevented him from going fishing on a nice, sunny afternoon. We have automated and made efficient—and time-efficient—all the operations. We have rendered things predictable. And, therefore, we have predicted the result. And all of this is necessary because we have invested our capital, because what is at stake is all that has been saved.

Two hundred years ago, when a man wove in woolens he wove from a loom in his own house, his own cottage. It was no great place to live. Let us not be foolish about that. Most workers went to the city as soon as they could, out of those cottages that we now admire in the British countryside. But anyway, when he wove, he wove, and when he felt like fishing, he fished, because there was nobody to tell him that time was of the utmost importance. And the reason nobody told him that was that he had had his loom for a hundred years, or five generations, and it was not capitalized. Then they built a factory, they spent huge sums on equipment, for which they had to borrow. And the moment they borrowed the money, they entered a race, a footrace, with production. The moment you borrow the money, you start paying interest. If you fail to get your tools in place and have more building to do, you cannot sell a pound of wool or charge for transporting a lump of coal. As you have the enterprise built and running you can start to charge, but not until then. So there is no way to pay off the interest, much less the principal, until you are in operation. Therefore, you must get into operation and run on time, day after day. Why? So that the money will come in; so that you can pay the interest; so that you can get the bank off your back; so that you can figure out new ways to expand; so that you can get new loans; so that you can run faster; so that you can get the bank off your back; so that you can expand capital. So *that*—so that *why?* I am not sure I know.

The grand symbol, of course, is the one that we know under the word *progress*. We call it "a rising standard of living for all." Decreased mortality. Better health. Increased choices for larger numbers of human beings. Yes, all of that—at a price that we pay in intense anxiety to keep everything moving. And in the process, the most prized person is the one who can juggle time like the juggler's balls in the air, who can move the elements about with ease and fluidity without dropping them, and who can keep things in motion until the time comes to say stop. It is now time to count and measure the progress of it all. In short, this person is a manipulator. That is not necessarily a testimony to evil. To manipulate is simply to handle, to move about, unless, of course, you conceal from others what you are handling and moving about without their permission.

Now, I am drawing here a caricature. We are describing management in some of its less lovely aspects: management that aims at control and impersonal objectivity, and that tries to keep things, insofar as possible, away from the peculiar and the unpredictable. It is not necessary to manage things that way, but that increasingly becomes the modus operandi of managers in our society because it cuts the number of variables. I ask my students, "What is the essence of the bureaucratic society?" And they say, "The essence of it is red tape." And I say, "Well, why is there red tape in a bureaucratic society?" And they say, "So people can be controlled, even if they complain." But that is, of course, to miss the point. The whole reason a bureaucratic society has red tape is that it must not operate at the level of mere personal decision in any matter whatsoever. One organizes the bureaucratic society for the specific purpose of taking human variables out of it and dealing only with constants. Ideally, one could finally submit the control of a society simply to the computer, properly programmed and to which we are all attached in some way, so that we might be monitored and profitably directed. It has nothing to do with our names. It has nothing to do with our places. It has nothing to do with our desires. It does not ask us. It simply relates us as elements in the cycle of production and consumption. If you want to speak, then, in the modern world about the possibilities of genuine dehumanization, this is as promising a place to look as any.

This can be and is being done with remarkable success in some churches. It may not be been done with much success in too many Covenant churches, perhaps because the people can be so craggy and peculiar that they are hard to fit into a slot. There are churches, however, where people are run in and out as though they were supermarket items with price tags on them. We have all seen them, on television, if nowhere else. There is a regular schedule and a prepackaged worship service, with calculated laughter here and weeping there, accompanied by the proper vibrato in the organ. There is, funds permitting, national coverage, and good-looking preachers who take care never to say anything very important, lest somebody get mad at them and disturb the careful routine of the service. Then the place is vacated and the next group ushered in. You can do that eight, ten times a Sunday, and accumulate quite a reputation for knowing how to make the church grow. And the poor salmon that they ship up and down these creeks, even if the leaders care, they hardly know what is happening to them at all in the particulars of their daily lives. They have just come up to spawn, and they go back down the runs again. It comforts some people to be put on a conveyor belt. And as long as there are enough people who do not object to being standardized in that way, which means a kind of manipulated prepackaging for the consumer, and even being told how to feel and behave, I suppose there is no reason why this should not succeed in a part of organized religion. I fail to see, however, why any person on an authentic Christian pilgrimage has to be treated like a migrating salmon or "smallfry" with their mouth open. I never have really quite understood that there is any connection between the two.

That is, to be made the object of other people's manipulation is not the infallible sign of advancing civilization. And there are ways of beating the game that are open to sensible men and women who are interested in being whole enough persons so they cannot really be prepackaged for anything. Of course, this does not make the job of management, along the standard lines of expectation, any easier for those who do not have that kind of cynical attitude toward the church or toward people in any public function. It rather makes it more difficult. For the more individual we become, the more uniquely and weightily personal we become, the less easy we are to push around or be conned, and the more difficult we are to manage.

Now, on the other hand, there would be a problem in the church and its ministry if all people were absolutely secure in themselves. They could not be made to feel guilty just because they did not participate in the congregation's life or had no sense of obligation (motivated by conscience) to support the work through the offering of their time, ability, and money. If that were the case, we might have some difficulty operating our *own* systems, since the manipulation of guilt is one of the devices by which the modern church is controlled. To manage guilt, whether the guilt is real or not, is a way of controlling personality and controlling public conduct. To threaten people subtly with a feeling of shame for being who they are offers possibilities for their manipulation, whether we use those possibilities consciously or unconsciously. This has been particularly true in conservative circles like ours, which have long since tied a vivid sense of the law and of the justice of God to the necessity of appearing weekly in church to get it off our backs. This only means that God is seen as a sort of weekly service-station attendant, who fills our pumps and cleans our windshields, a service that needs to be repeated frequently for anyone on a journey. Even this now is self-service.

Some of this is, of course, only a suggestion for critical reflection, and I do not want to be heard as saying something between the lines, which is more than I mean to imply. Yet if it is the true and historic mission of the church, finally, to release people in God's name from the burden of guilt they carry, then it ought to be our obligation to try and arrange the church in such a way that they never need to carry a burden of guilt for the purposes of manipulating their behavior. This means that any sense of guilt and shame is profoundly linked to our sinfulness in relation to the God whom we praise and serve.

The manager rightfully labors hard to preserve capital and be responsible in all matters, whether financial or metaphorical. We understand that the planter is given the seed, has no control over the environment, and is lucky to get a crop. We congratulate him or her if there is any crop at all, against those odds. But we insist that the manager show results. I once spoke with a young minister who was in a New England town, in a practically moribund church, where the population of the town was 98 percent Roman Catholic. He was visited by one of his denominational leaders, who, without regard for context, told him, "If I were here, I'd have increased this membership by 15 percent in a month." "Well," said this young minister, "I could go out and club them on the head, too, but I don't think that's the way you want things done."

The *mood* is what I am after, what we expect of ourselves, even if no one else expects it. I mean our self-image, which makes us feel that we are responsible for performance, and that when something goes wrong, it is our fault. It is because we have been lazy. It is because we have not paid attention to detail. It is because we have not taken a course in management. It is because we do not have the right symbols in our image, the right logo on our publicity. Or, if we are feeling sorry for ourselves and we want to project the problem, it is because all the other people in the church are problematic and cannot be made to see the vision of the Christian life. Somebody has to be blamed. But what if the blame is to be taken by God himself? What if it is God's fault? What if it is? What if God has decided, in his infinite humor, that he does not want it to grow there? Can we face that? It is one of the characteristics of our management consciousness, however, that we know exactly what God wants, namely 18.5 percent a year, compounded. And we can footnote it and program it to happen.

Now, we cannot be caught in quite that obvious a trap. Of course God wants growth. But if we say, "Of course God wants growth," we are talking about an abstraction. We are not speaking about the God of Abraham, Isaac, and Jacob, and the Father of our Lord Jesus Christ, who is making extremely personal decisions and is not afraid of confounding us with the personality and the apparent contradictions of his decisions. He gives growth as he pleases. He sends the rain and the sun as he pleases. And the most insidious danger we face as managers in this kind of civilization is ultimately the erosion of his sovereignty in the face of our subtle control over the categories in which we express our own self-glorification.

I know it is always possible to cop out and say, "Well, if God had wanted it to grow, he would have made it grow. It's not my fault." But we know in all honesty when we are copping out. We know as well when we have done all that could be done. Our people in the churches for the most part know it. And there is no point in trying to give God an education in what he ought to do for the Covenant Church. It is like the old saying about people sailing in the "Roaring Forties" around Cape Horn: "He who sails around Cape Horn and spits into the wind spits into his own face." And the one who tries to give instructions to God about his purposes is reaping a whirlwind, or at least an awfully appropriate comeuppance of some kind or another. In this, we are accepting the categories of the general secular civilization. Whatever else we might say about the achievements of the modern technological age (in living standard, in progress for the people of the world, in the efficient use of energy, and in all the rest of it), we cannot say is that all this has led to the deepening and enriching of the human personality. That is not the way things are done. And the reason for it is that the human personality is too unpredictable and too sovereign. It is understood to be an end in itself, in conflict with the other ends that are supposed to ensure the expansion of all of that credit, and the expenditure of all of that energy. If the ultimate beatitude of human beings is that they should become what God originally envisioned them to be, in all of his full, weighty glory, then they will look as little like a machine as it is possible to look.

But we are a gadget-conscious society, and we love them! On every university and college campus in the country today there is a crisis of conscience going on. Everybody has a computer. They are marvelous instruments that can count all sorts of things faster than one can think. In nanoseconds they can count the distances of stars. Most of us may not know how, but they can do it. And if you want to calculate intricate trajectories to put people on the moon, there is nothing like it. Despite the fact that these things are everywhere on the campus and are humming all the time, they do not seem to be accomplishing anything. It bothers people. So presidents and directors of financial operations are sending down directives: "Think of something for the machine to do." And most faculty members send back notes that say, "We tell the machine what to do: unplug itself and take a vacation." But you cannot do it because of the tremendous investment in the machine, and you must be able to tell your board of directors that all computers are used 85 percent of the time, otherwise they will be judged to be an extravagant waste. So you put brilliant people to work making it count things. And they invent new languages, counting things that really ought never to be counted, and putting garbage in so you can get garbage out. But it is being used. So the president is happy, and the director of financial operations is happy, and the board of directors is happy, and the thing is chirping merrily away, and lights are flashing all over the place, and all sorts of people are kept from going fishing to keep that thing going.

Now it is really obvious that I am caricaturing our situation. On a more limited scale, however, we have exactly that sort of thing going on in our churches as well. We have what is called "lay utilization." You sit down with your membership books and you conclude, "This guy's not doing anything, and this one isn't doing anything, and this one isn't doing anything." And you have been told that the way to get church growth is to use the laity. The minute lay people get involved and start doing things, they get good feelings about the church, because they are doing things for the church and that ties them to it. So let us find out things for them to do. And you burn the midnight oil, as managers, to find out things for your laity to do. You call them up and say: "You know, it just occurred to me . . ." Or you do it three steps removed, through the chair of the deacons or somebody else, and have them say to the guy that by spending a weekend with the Cub Scouts up at Camp Gitcheegoomie, he could fill his life with joy. His washing machine is broken down, he needs to tune his car, and he ought to remake his acquaintance with his wife, but he needs to do something for the church, so out he goes with the scouts to Gitcheegoomie.

He is being manipulated. He is not really being used; he is just being plugged in and keeping his lights flashing. It is garbage in and garbage out. He may learn something in the process. It may conceivably be of some value for him to do what he is doing; he may meet a kid in the process. I do not declare that all scout activity is useless, or anything of the sort. You must understand me better than that. Our efforts to get people involved, and to keep them involved like so many balls being juggled in the air, does not necessarily mean that the will of God is being accomplished. It may only mean a flurry of activity, with phones ringing and lights flashing, and be divorced from the reality of meaningful lay ministry. In fact, God may be bored by the whole thing.

If we are to believe the vision of God that we have in our Bibles, we know that he is supremely the master of reality. He is supremely the creator of a cosmos in which awesome wonders are on daily display. Because of our pressures in life, and our constant self-examination, as well as our need to perform, we never take the time to *see* these wonders. It is as one of my students said last week, "I've made an important discovery: you don't see much of the world when you're constantly examining your navel." I got up right out of my chair and shouted, "Hallelujah! Another convert!" Somebody is going to look *out* at the world! Somebody is going to *look* at these mountains! Somebody is going actually to look at human beings and *see* them with all their majestic potential of becoming citizens of a city not made with hands. Somebody is going to see them, not as elements in production, but as creatures of the new creation. Somebody is going to see them as the poetry of God's heaven, and say, "I don't care about the schedule. Let's go have coffee. I want to hear what you have to say." Somebody is going to live with them in depth, and is going to touch and be touched by them, and is going to be raised by them and get a taste of what blessedness really is going to be like. In short, somebody is going to begin to live in the world of God's creation as it ultimately will be, right *now*. And out of that somebody is going to gather the strength to be able to say to the garbage-in-garbage-out syndrome, "I'm sorry, I don't have time for that kind of stuff. I'm engaged in *real enterprises*. There are *real* things I want to do." If our programs and techniques of management prevent this from happening, they must be gotten rid of or reevaluated for the sake of the gospel and the church's ministry.

I think of managing, in its best sense, in the images we have of Jesus as a manager. It is almost laughable to use those words in conjunction, I suppose. There was a book not long ago that portrayed Jesus as an international business executive. He took twelve men from the bottom ranks of business and forged them into an organization that conquered the world. If he lived today, he would be an international advertiser. Billboards, you know—the sayings of Jesus on billboards. It seemed foolish at the time, but there is this element of truth in it: Jesus apparently looked so intently at particular people that he saw things in them that no one else saw. *No one* else saw. He approaches a scum of a tax collector who has been conning and scamming his fellow citizens all his life. This is a man utterly without principles, so far as anybody can tell, quite capable of throwing people out of their homes. Jesus looks through him, and, without more than a few words of conversation, orders him to come and follow him. And he turns him into a gospel writer. That is managing—to be able to look at something so thoroughly, so finally, and so accurately that you see its potential all the way into blessedness. To be able to be an agent of a person's liberation and growth, is to be a manager. This is what we are meant to do for each other—to liberate each other in the name of Jesus. Not to press each other into columns, not to cram each other into stereotypical forms, but to organize and inspire each other to become what God made us to be, and to trust that vision in each of us.

Now, I dare to say that you cannot do that with millions of people at once. Not even Jesus did it with millions of people at once. He did it with one at a time. That is why I like it that we are a comparatively small denomination. It is to our advantage as we desire to grow in authentic ways, because as long as we are smaller and, therefore, more relationally based, there is less danger of losing perspective on management or misplacing its role. It also breeds humility. In short, it is still possible to be human, and to live on a human scale. The more I see of mass, the more I see of sheer power, the more I see of sheer weight, and the more I see of stellar distances, the happier I am for my own garden. I share in the spirit of Henry David Thoreau, who, when asked why he did not tour Europe, said, "I have traveled the world extensively in Concord." And the one who is capable of looking deeply into one's own garden has perhaps seen more of the world than most eyes have seen. Anyone who has experienced true fellowship in the company of one's brothers and sisters in Christ has probably had more fellowship than the masses of people who bounce off each other like smooth billiard balls in the constant interactions and clicks and clacks of the mass society that surrounds them.

We are not merely a freeway society. We still have much about us in the nature of our church that is horse and buggy. We are not spinning at seventy-five miles an hour, down in our alligator carapaces, belching smog all over the world. We are still horse-and-buggy people, clattering along to the song of Old Dobbin, and a little backward perhaps in the eyes of the modern world. It is not that we *could not* do other things. We have the intelligence, devotion, and the gifted people to do it. I think there is a kind of suspicion that the slick cult of bigness and smoothness is not really going to turn out what people want it to be. That is, it is not going to produce what it is the destiny of the church to be.

One ought to manage also so that at the crucial moment when it is time to deny the institution itself for the sake of the kingdom, one is free to do so. In any choice between the church and the kingdom, the kingdom has to win, even if you are the servants of the kingdom by being duly anointed as servants of the church. If the orders come to uproot, you must obey the orders and march. Even if it is not in the schedule. Even if it is not on the computer. Even if you do not want to. You are going to have to march whether you want to or not. Our history tells us that if you do not march one way, God will find another way to get you moving. Instead of building as though we were going to be in a particular place a thousand years, we must feel free to live in tents, and to meet each other by the campfire, if that is what is called for. I do not predict that that is what is we will be called to do. It is not an assertion. I am saying, however, that our sense of management must wait upon the prior will of God, and must take those forms in a sensible and human way that seem available to us, as honest men and women, to do God's work.

And for the rest of it, to go home and *sleep* quietly, and leave it to God. We pray every day, "Our Father, thy will be done on earth as it is in heaven." And then we stay awake all night for fear that he cannot do it, or will not do it, or that he might need more information. I have done that, and it is just plumb silly. It does not fit with what we already believe. They asked Franklin Roosevelt whether in the burden of the war he had had many sleepless nights. He said, only one: the night Winston Churchill called him and said, "I think Britain will go down tonight." You cannot blame a man for staying awake on a night like that. "Otherwise," he said, "I just told myself, 'Well, Franklin, you've made some and you've lost some today. But whether you did a good job or a bad job, it's over, and there isn't a blessed thing you can gain by sitting around grumbling about it, so go to sleep.'" Now, there is no particular faith in that. That is just good old farmers' common sense. But with faith added to it, the conviction that, despite everything—and this is God's last humor—*he uses us* to do his purposes in the world.

Is that good news? I guess it is! Do we really mean it? Or is there an unregenerate corner of our spirits that says, "Yes, but, you know, God is really very old fashioned. He hasn't seen the newest mainframe IBM 360s, and he doesn't yet know what they can do. Now, if I could get Trinitarian theology on that mainframe and check it out, we could go from 18.5 percent compounded growth rate to 22.5 percent inside three and a half years, or at least 3.56." Is that not dumb? But that is the way we think. Because there is something reserved in the corner of us that says, "He cannot be trusted, finally, to work out his own purposes. He cannot be trusted to defend himself. We must constantly be defending him against his enemies. We must constantly be sustaining him, we must constantly be careful of his reputation, lest he lose the battle. The prince of darkness is very strong."

I will tell you the story I have told many times about my own liberation. It was during the time of my first sabbatical, in 1965. I came home from Christmas vacation, and sat down in the living room on the first day of my sabbatical. I had two terms off to do nothing but read. But I was soon afflicted by the thought that I was not needed after all.

I waited for the telephone to ring, because I was sure that about two hours into the first day of term they would call up and say, "Zenos, I know we gave you a sabbatical, I know that we guaranteed you six months off, but we can't do it. You must come back." And I would say, "You people are impossible. It's all right. Don't worry. I'll come back." And I would love every minute of it. But the phone did not ring, then or in the days that followed. I spent the most absurd week with myself. I would walk slowly back and forth in front of the administration building, with a book in my hand so they would know I was reading, you know. Yet I hoped they would run out and say, "You have to come back!" They did not even *look* at me! And I got grumpy and jumpy. I got short with my wife, until finally she took me by the arm and said, "Look. Either you snap out of it or you move out for the whole rest of this time, because I'm not going to put up with this!" She said, "What is the matter with you?" And I said, "Well, I, you know . . . " I had to admit, there was something the matter with me. It was that they did not need me. The school was continuing. I was not indispensable. And then, of course, there dawned on me a sense of liberation so overwhelming, a sense of freedom. I could contribute, but I was not indispensable.

In its proper perspective, managing means keeping order in a chaotic world while recognizing that there is no more control over what is managed than there was for our predecessors who were uprooted, who planted, and who fenced. Like them, the manager cannot ultimately answer for the final outcome because its creation and control is beyond us. The manager says: "All I can do is be as faithful a steward as I can. If you can show me how to be more faithful without ceasing to be myself, and without running the mortal danger of misunderstanding the nature of my responsibility and of losing my freedom as a child of God, I will be glad to accept what instruction you have to offer. But do not give me gimmicks! Do not con me. Do not give me the universal solvent. Do not try and sell me the Brooklyn Bridge of management. Do not give me training courses or tie me impersonally into the computer. Do not do anything to me that I cannot live with as a fully-grown human being among other fully-grown human beings who are put into my charge and into my care and to whom I am fundamentally committed. I want nothing coming between us. No guarantees. I want no guarantees or simple formulas for growth—unless it is given by *his* will and under *his* authority and by *his* power. And if you are willing to let me be a minister of Christ under these circumstances, I will give you everything I have, but nothing more. I will give you all my devotion; I will give you all my authenticity; and I will give you all the spirit and prayer that I can muster. But I demand my freedom as a human being, my authority as a child of Christ, and my right to meet my fellow human beings in that freedom."

Even in our complex world, I believe that it *is* possible to manage under those terms. Good management comes from uncomplicated and faithful stewards, and will be rewarded by the king when he returns with the words, "Good and faithful servant!" I do not know what he is going to say to the computer. I suspect that what he will do is stand back, put his hands on his hips, and have a belly laugh. When I seek a way of expressing the pilgrim life, I take it to be a life, which sooner or later, has this delicious sense that it is not ultimately at home here, though it is here temporarily in all of its rich fullness in Christ.

CHAPTER 5

The Pilgrim Psalm

A sermon preached April 20, 1978, at Arvada, Colorado

T onight is the eve of Passover. And on Seder tables in the homes of the children of Israel all over the world, Father asks the ancient question: "Why is this night different from every other night in the year?" And if you will quiet your spirits before that question, I should like to read to you briefly from the pilgrim psalm, Psalm 107.

> *O give thanks to the Lord, for he is good;*
>   *for his steadfast love endures forever.*
> *Let the redeemed of the Lord say so,*
>   *those he redeemed from trouble*
> *and gathered in from the lands,*
>   *from the east and from the west,*
>   *from the north and from the south.*
>
> *Some wandered in desert wastes,*
>   *finding no way to an inhabited town;*
> *hungry and thirsty,*
>   *their soul fainted within them.*
> *Then they cried to the Lord in their trouble,*
>   *and he delivered them from their distress;*
> *he led them by a straight way,*
>   *until they reached an inhabited town.*
> *Let them thank the Lord for his steadfast love,*
>   *for his wonderful works to humankind.*
> *For he satisfies the thirsty,*
>   *and the hungry he fills with good things.*

> Some sat in darkness and in gloom,
>> prisoners in misery and in irons,
> for they had rebelled against the words of God,
>> and spurned the counsel of the Most High.
> Their hearts were bowed down with hard labor;
>> they fell down, with no one to help.
> Then they cried to the Lord in their trouble,
>> and he saved them from their distress;
> he brought them out of darkness and gloom,
>> and broke their bonds asunder.
> Let them thank the Lord for his steadfast love,
>> for his wonderful works to humankind.

You and I, of course, are accustomed, because of our long and careful biblical training, to recognize the hand of God in the history of the people Israel. Jews tonight are remembering the terror and the expectation of the night when the angel of the Lord flamed across Egypt. The firstborn of the Egyptians were about to die, and the Jews were gathering their belongings for the great pilgrimage to freedom. We recognize God's hand in their liberation from Egypt, in their terrified progress across the Red Sea, in the long and painful and troublesome wandering in the desert, and in their coming to the Promised Land. So that when the Jewish father tonight recalls that night of terror, he is recalling to them the faithfulness of their God—and ours. Why, indeed, is this night different from every other night?

And so it may be in our own history, for we too are a Passover people. Our fathers and mothers had been uprooted by God's hand stirring in history, taken from the places where they had lived—they and their parents before them for centuries beyond memory—and flung out of their pleasant places into a wild and chaotic world of strange languages, peoples, and customs, where security was unknown. Our parents, too, were torn out of all that was familiar, out of all that had made them who they were—by forces that they only dimly perceived and seldom understood. Our spiritual parents in the Covenant Church, too, became wanderers across stormy seas, carrying their pathetic little sea chests, all that remained of the old life—a handful of clothes, a piece of needlework, a pot or a pan, a copper kettle, and hope. And our parents, too, searched for a city not made with hands, for a haven from the storm, for land from which to feed their children, for space in which their spirits could expand, for the possibility of new life in new dignity. And if it is possible for the Lord God to move the children of Israel from Egypt, then it is possible for the Lord God to move the children of Europe to America.

And it is in the understanding of the meaning and significance of that question that we are, in a sense, met here tonight to ask, "What continues to be the mission of our people?" What was the significance of our uprooting? For what reason did God bring us here? What did he want us to do? Today, in a society that is high-pressure, high-power, abstract, and bureaucratic, it is possible for Christians to have become so separated from their own particular and familial sense of purpose that they no longer see the larger choices and struggles in life except as an immediate response to the pressures of the moment. Those who first spread out over this vast frontier did so with a sense of purpose. They were looking for land. They were looking for a city. They were looking for a home. They were looking for a future. And that "looking-for" protected them from purposelessness, as our property does not. For we, as their children, have inherited their hope. We have realized their dream, and we have it in the bank at six percent interest. And tonight on the evening of Passover, that is the question I want to put to you. What about the pilgrim dream?

What was it like in the world of our parents in Europe? To live with a family of five or seven on what could be produced from eleven acres of stony, rocky land, with a short growing season, with bad seed, with all the nutrition that almost pure sand can supply, plenty of water but not enough substance? What was it like to live where your children are perpetually hungry? What was it like to live where you live in a caste from which you have no real hope of escape because education is reserved for the children of the nobility and of the upper-middle class? What was it like to live in a land where the church is controlled by the aristocracy, and where it is the function of ordinary people to bow and to scrape, to accept and to be quiet? What was it like to live in that kind of land when suddenly you feel that you and your children, your spouse, your parents, and your hope for the future is surplus? There is no place for you. There is no need for you. You are, in fact, an embarrassment.

Such a man was Carl Johan Nyvall. He was a perfectly ordinary boy in a Swedish province, whose father was an iron-molder, whose mother was a distraught housewife, not quite sure that she should have been married to this wild character, and feeling in her bones in the mid-1840s the darkness of the life that surrounded her. As it turned out, thousands of other Swedes felt the same. And with this feeling of incompleteness, with this feeling of contradiction and emptiness swirling like a dark fog inside of her, she went looking for the only help she could find—to the younger pastor in the state church congregation, who counseled her and another woman. Maria Nilsdotter, Carl Johan's mother, and Birgitta Olsson, the mother of Olof Olsson (who became a pioneer pastor-settler in Lindsborg, Kansas, and president of Augustana College), were advised by the pastor to sit down together weekly, and more often if possible, to read. To read what? To read the Bible. To read Luther's homilies. To read a new magazine from Stockholm that was just now appearing, called *Pietisten* (The Pietist), with its monthly sermon. These women had no education. They had no voice in Swedish society. They had only this terrible internal hunger, which translated the earthquake shocks of the earth into their spirits and cried for release. And they read for years, until they found it possible to believe the good news that was coming from *Pietisten*—that is, from the gospel through this evangelical magazine. God is not your judge, said this good news. God is your loving Father. He has been looking for you all along. You do not have to change for him to forgive you. He wants you now. And they believed it.

And in the darkness of the forest in the province of Värmland there glowed a light, which began to spread to the children of these devout women, uneducated as they were. Young Carl Johan was a wild adolescent, out on the family horse until two o'clock every morning, out on the frontiers between Örebro and Karlskoga, fighting the Örebro boys—gang rumbles in the rural Swedish countryside. And saying innocently to his mother in the morning, when she saw the horse standing lathered in the stall, "He must have been ridden by spooks." In short, he was a strong, vital boy, who one day out in the woods, having been preached to by his mother and having evaded her successfully so far, slipped with the axe, laid open the calf of his leg to the bone, and severed a major artery. The only available physician, the midwife, stitched the artery together and compressed the wound. For eight weeks he lay between life and death. He later said, "Oh, how I prayed in the night: 'At the very least, don't let me die before you save me!' "

It gets dark in those forests—and then there came light. And he joined his mother's circle, the cell. Carl Johan began to read in the cell. And out of the reading came a conviction that he could help as a book-seller, so he was sent to Stockholm, providing him an opportunity to sell books for one crown a month. That was about two bits. Even in 1856, that was not much. But neither was he, because when they saw him in Stockholm, they said, "Well, you look pretty dumb and bashful to us. But we're not exactly overwhelmed with applicants, so maybe you might as well try." And he did try. And it may encourage some of the more timid among us to have his frank confession: "I took every back trail I knew with my sack of books to avoid meeting anybody I knew, because I was embarrassed to talk to them." He said, "I didn't make a very good sales talk for my Savior." He got a backache, so he got a horse. But they made him get off his horse, because if you came by horse, you were a preacher, and he was only a bookseller. And then he said, "I can't carry this thing with my bad back. What do I care what they say? If the Lord calls me a preacher, that's one thing. I'm just a bookseller."

So he got back on the horse, and then began a career of forty years, during which time he became, in effect, the great free church bishop of the whole northwest of Sweden. Three years of elementary school education was all he managed to get. He always thought of himself as an ordinary man. He always apologized for his preaching, though he thought he sang pretty well. And when in 1878 they formed the Covenant in Sweden, and when in 1885 they organized the Covenant in America, Carl Johan Nyvall was there both times. Where had he come from? Not from the theological faculty at the university. Who had qualified him? The ordinary people of the district in which he lived. Who supported him? The people of the cells, the ordinary Swedish people gathered to read, to sing, to evangelize, and to nurture one another. The darkness? Yes, the storm was still there. But in the middle of the storm had appeared hope. In the middle of the storm had appeared liberation.

Consider the case of a young cobbler in Småland named Carl August Björk. A heavy-handed man, he was tall and big-fisted. He had become an apprentice at the age of eleven. Then he served his hitch in the army, where he took the name Björk. It means birch tree. He returned and established his own cobbling shop with his own appren-tices, and beat them on the ears when they failed do what they were supposed to do. In the same town lived a little tailor and others who had a cell. And whenever he, the cobbler, went by the tailor shop, the tailor would say, "We're having a meeting tonight. Why don't you come?" And Björk would flex his great muscles and say, "No way!" One afternoon the tailor became especially direct with him. "Björk, you're frightened of coming." "I'm not frightened at all of coming. I'm two of you," said he. And he was. The tailor was just a little fellow. "What time is the meeting?" And he came, his whole frame tensed up, ready to take him on. And the cell gathered, and in its quiet way read the sermon, read some passages from Luther's Small Catechism, and Björk sat there ready to fight. And nobody paid him the slightest attention.

Now, these people had never read Dale Carnegie. These were folk psychologists, filled with the love of Jesus. They knew their man. They had been aiming at him with the flaming arrows of the Lord's angel for years. And when the meeting broke up and dismissed with a quiet prayer, Björk stood bewildered. "You invited me. There was going to be a fight," his silent posture said. Instead, the little tailor came up to him and, reaching his hand way up on Björk's shoulder, with tears running down his cheeks and onto his white beard, said simply, "Poor little Björk. Poor little Björk." And the big man dissolved and went back privately to his own room and gave it up, and committed himself. And the next night, when he was due to be the *spelman* (the fiddler) at the dance in the local tavern, Björk went, found his whole crowd there—he was the leader—raised the fiddle, smashed it on his knee, and said, "Now. There's a meeting at the schoolhouse. We're all going." Saul of Tarsus has become Paul—in Småland, in Sweden.

Shortly thereafter, in 1864, Carl August Björk packed up his cobbling tools, grabbed his satchel and his sea chest, and made his way by sailing ship across the stormy Atlantic into the St. Lawrence River. Shipwrecked on Anticosti Island, he made his way down the Great Lakes to Chicago, and by train to Moline, and by stagecoach to Des Moines, and by foot to a place called Swede Bend, with the commendable, elegant simplicity of the frontier. There was a bend in the river and there were Swedes there. Hence Swede Bend. And there he took his place as a reader of *Pietisten*, just as though he had been in Småland. And here Björk discovered anew that the ground was shaking as well, and that there was gospel in it. From there, he would go to Chicago in 1878 as the leader of the Mission Synod, and in 1885 he became the first president of the Covenant Church.

Let me give you one other example. In 1876, there came to Chicago, late on a hot, dusty summer afternoon after two-and-a-half days on the train from New York, windows wide open and therefore soot-drenched, a young Swedish preacher named Erik August Skogsbergh. Less than five-and-a-half feet tall, almost on tiptoes, 120 pounds sopping wet, a sparrow of a man yet incandescent with energy, Skogsbergh had been accumulating a reputation among the Mission Friends in Sweden as a preacher. The Americans in Chicago, who now had a mission society eight years old, thought, "This is the man for us," and called him—once, twice, refused each time, and on the third time finally, worn out but challenged, he consented. Now, much against every inclination in his own spirit, he was sitting in that railroad station of his final destination, after this long journey from Sweden, surrounded by the chaos of the central Chicago district, hot, hungry, dusty, tired, alone—utterly alone. He was greeted by a little man with a tall stove-pipe hat knocked askew on one corner, with his tie under one ear. He never could get his tie where it belonged. The colporteur of the Swedish Mission Society of Chicago, J. M. Sanngren, met him in his car, said, "Aha! You're Skogsbergh? Come with me. You're preaching tonight." A very formal invitation. "You're preaching tonight." This was the young hotshot from Sweden, who now, weary and covered with soot from head to toe, no clean clothes, was preaching that night, to validate or invalidate the choice the Mission Friends had made, sight unseen, from across the sea.

They whisked him down to Franklin Street and dumped him in an iron bathtub; they gave him clean linen and got him dressed; they led him to the Swedish-American table, which was already groaning with the weight of the food piled on it, and made him eat. And all this time his head was bursting: "What is my text? What is my text?" All preachers take note! He later said of himself that when he had been in P. A. Ahlberg's missionary training school in Småland, he had picked a very complicated text from 1 Peter because he was too good for the simpler texts. And when he had appeared in the pulpit, he had forgotten it all. And now, perhaps remembering this, he was desperate; but there is something authentic about the solution to which he finally came. He was then led to the little Franklin Street church, which was filled to the rafters with people and was already as hot as, he called it, "my Finnish bathhouse." During the service, he was seated directly behind Sanngren, who was known to be excitable. Skogsbergh wrote in his memoirs that on one occasion Sanngren kicked back like a mule, almost hitting him in the face. He always sat to one side after that. But on that first evening Skogsbergh looked at all those hungry, expectant faces, those people who were anticipating from him a miracle of performance. And he had nothing to say. He did not even have a text, much less an outline. And finally the last song had been sung, he had been introduced, he had to stand up, he had now arrived. He still had no text, except one word— one word, Jesus. And that became his sermon. One word—Jesus. Not for nostalgic purposes, not for lack of anything else, but because he had been driven back to the rock.

In the storm, that is what our spiritual parents had learned. "Great hills may tremble and mountains may crumble," sings Lina Sandell. But the love of Jesus is forever—the love of Jesus and the fellowship of Jesus's sheep. Forgiveness and fellowship distilled from the suffering, from the wandering, from the uncertainty, from the insecurity. When you have lived for 500 years in a single culture, and when it is a traditional culture and it defines everything you do, and suddenly you are ripped out of that culture, how do you live? You live with Jesus, in the fellowship, accepting the discipline of your common commitment, but, above all, accepting the necessity of obedience to him. All the conflict about the atonement, all the conflict about the communion table, all the conflict about the final definition of the meaning of the congregation—it all boils down finally to this: do you love Jesus? Are you willing to obey him? Are you willing to be our brother and sister as we also try to obey him? That is the rock. That is the minimum that can be said, around which all the old stories can be woven. And that is what our forebears learned in the middle of the storm. They learned much, much more, but that they knew by experience.

And now I come to ask you, to ask all of us who are the inheritors of this tradition: do you think you own all this? Do you think it belongs to you? Have you done it? Can this remain the adhesive within an increasingly diverse church? I want to ask you about your horizons. But before I ask you about your horizons, I want to say something to you that I am reticent to say because it opens me to difficulty, and I say it with fear and trembling. The revolution out of which our tradition came has not ended; it is accelerating. The movement of those forty million Europeans to the North American continent was only the beginning. There is no place on the globe today that can stand secure and changeless. It is all changing. It is changing before our eyes. No one can predict what will happen to global culture in even the near future. If you have come out of the pilgrim tradition of the children of Israel, from Egypt to the Promised Land, and have used that magnificent opportunity only to become a Philistine, then take heed. Do you live comfortably behind high walls and bronzed gates, and worship regularly at the altar of Baal? Are you pleased with the prospects of Social Security and a special pension plan, or the apparent security of America's nuclear deterrent and the overwhelming power of its society and technology? If that provides comfort, then live in fear and trembling, because it will all be taken away from you as surely as was the security of our forebears. I proclaim it.

The Egyptians who sat this night long ago knew nothing of the angel of the Lord with his flaming sword. Only those who had been told knew it—the slaves, the children of Israel, preparing for their departure. For Egyptians it was a night like any night in the year. Only in the morning would they discover their terror. The children of this earth do not understand their danger, for they believe in these things. They believe in their bombs. They believe in Fort Knox and the dollar. They believe in mortgages and segregated suburbs and high technology, and all the elegant gadgets with which we congratulate ourselves upon our immortality and our cleverness, the toys with which we while away our adult time and pretend that we control history.

Was it to make Philistines of us that our Covenant forebears were led from Europe? Was it simply to provide us with a horizon no more distant than our own retirement? Is an interest in compassion, in the progress of the world, no more distant than an easy charity, with a willingness to sacrifice only when the "sacrifice" can offer a public relations return or a tax deduction? Are we so constrained by a careful, anxious middle-class consciousness that if we do not take care of ourselves, no one else will? That is the talk of the Philistine. The Lord shook the earth for a purpose. And in the shaking of the earth he revealed to us the good news, that when we liberate our spirits to the life of pilgrimage, all joy worth having becomes our own—absolutely, absolutely for nothing. You cannot pay for it. It is priceless.

I appeal to you on this Passover night. Whatever this means to you as a member of your church, as a member of our larger fellowship, and ultimately the whole Church (because all pilgrims finally come to recognize all fellow pilgrims on the high road of Christ's destiny), I appeal to you: do not sit, in your spirit, any longer in Egypt. The angel with his flaming sword is not deterred by walls, is not impressed by the U.S. Air Force. There is no defense that human beings can build against him. Gather your spirit instead with the pilgrims of old within the doors marked for your safety by the blood of the Lamb, the spotless Lamb without blemish. For as the angel goes overhead seeking his prey, you will be spared for the pilgrim way. And in the quiet of that room and of our fellowship here, in some deep recess of your own soul, as the angel of the Lord flashes over to do his historic destiny, listen in silence for the command of the risen Shepherd. Our forebears obeyed him. And you and I have joy here tonight, nourished by the roots by which they found nourishment, because of their decision.

If we are to leave a tradition for our children, we must commit ourselves in the same decision. In this way lies freedom. You can be a pilgrim, you know, and never move. It is a question of what you are ready for. And if your bag is packed, the Lord may not call today or tomorrow or even thirty years from now; but he sees it packed. And if you are ready to go when he calls you, you are a pilgrim, and you are welcome— to our song and to our fireside, and to the blessedness that is in store on the other side of the river. Amen.

II

PIETISM AND THE COVENANT EXPERIENCE

CHAPTER 6

Reflections on Our Experience of Pietism

Address at Salem Covenant Church, May 8, 1987
New Brighton, Minnesota

I n late 1841, George Scott proposed to establish a devotional journal to communicate with the increasing numbers of Swedes interested in his ministry, and to call it *Pietisten* (The Pietist). For more than eleven years Scott had been the English Methodist pastor of the Bethlehem Chapel in Stockholm. Having recently returned from a fundraising tour of the United States, Scott reported:

> The Archbishop of that day [Carl F. Wingård] approved of my project, but urged me not to think of issuing a journal with so obnoxious a name; assuring me that, although he much wished to encourage the enterprise, he could not even have on his table a paper bearing a title used in the country as a byword of reproach. I could not, however, see my way to an alteration, and many a time since have I been thankful that I did not consent to change the title.[1]

Not for nothing was the archbishop disturbed. "The word 'Pietist' became more than a name. It became a program and a banner."[2] Scott, the target of a bitter xenophobic campaign in the Swedish press, was forced to leave the country in the spring of 1842, but his work was more secure than perhaps he knew in the hands of his Swedish assistant, the twenty-six-year-old Carl Olof Rosenius, of whom Scott said:

> I gratefully received him as a fellow helper, not expecting him to become a Methodist, but rather rejoicing that he, as a Lutheran, could command an amount of influence amongst Lutherans not possessed by Christians of other churches. . . .

Holding clean and strong views, agreeing with my own as to
the way of salvation by faith in Christ, the necessity of the new
birth, and of personal holiness, and being earnestly desirous of
saving souls from death, we two (the Methodist and the
Lutheran) worked together not only in perfect harmony but
with an ardor of mutual affection similar to that subsisting
between David and Jonathan.[3]

THE FORCES OF THE SEED

What was this Pietism? What was its program and why was it a
banner to which increasing numbers of Christians would rally? The name
itself seems to have originated with Philipp Jakob Spener (1635-1705),
pastor in Frankfurt, Dresden, and Berlin, an ardent and unrepentant
Lutheran. He had devoted his main energies to the reform and renewal
of the German churches, experimenting with the establishment of
devotional and instructional conventicles (*collegia pietatis*) in his Frankfurt congregation. In 1675, Spener wrote an introduction entitled "Pia
Desideria" to a new edition of Johan Arndt's popular sermons on the
appointed Gospels of the church year (originally published in 1615), in
which he argued for six necessary changes in church practice:

1) That there must be "a more extensive use of the Word
of God among us." Preaching must become more biblical than
theological. Families must practice daily Bible reading and study.
Christians must share in biblical exposition and discussion, suit-
ably in the conventicle.

2) That there must be a return to Luther in the matter of
the "establishment and diligent exercise of the spiritual priesthood" by all Christians. Unless the laity accept responsibility
for Christian ministration, the church will be dead.

3) That "knowledge of the Christian faith [is not enough],
for Christianity consists rather of practice." Pastors and laity
alike must be motivated to good works in the name of Christ.

4) That we "beware how we conduct ourselves in religious
controversies with unbelievers and heretics." Christians should
encounter opponents in the collegial spirit of the Good
Samaritan.

5) That pastors be trained in piety as well as theology, in practical ministry as well as in erudition.

6) That the purpose of preaching is "that [faith and its fruits] may be achieved in the hearers to the greatest possible degree."[4]

How entirely natural, how like breathing itself these proposals sound to all of us! That is because the movement of which Spener was part is now widely recognized as comprising the main thrust of modern Protestantism. This includes a complex set of developments stretching from devotional Puritanism in Britain to Reformed and Lutheran Pietism on the continent and in Scandinavia, and including John Wesley and the indigenous frontier churches of North America.[5] Martin Buber has made us aware that the creation of Hasidism in eighteenth-century Eastern Europe was a peculiarly parallel development in Judaism. Not surprisingly, Hasids were known as Jewish Pietists.[6] There are even those who recognize in French Jansenism a Pietist movement in the Roman Catholic communion.[7]

In Spener's time these transformations lay well in the dim and unpredictable future. He himself looked longingly forward to "better times in the church," but he and his successors lived in heated tension with their ecclesiastical contemporaries who saw them as troublemakers, visionaries, and heretics, potential if not actual. The establishment (Catholic, Protestant, and Jewish) really did not need more troubles than they already had.

We need to understand the social situation of the seventeenth and eighteenth centuries. What the reformers seem to have desired by way of religious change was not exactly what they got. In England, Henry VIII financed his royal power by plundering the monastic orders, creating the Church of England, and placing himself at its head. Luther exploded: "This king wants not only to be king but pope as well!" In Sweden, Gustaf Vasa built royal castles all over the land, using chapter houses as quarries. German princes arrogated power to themselves as heads of state and heads of church, and by the treaty of Westphalia (1648) claimed the power *cujus regio, ejus religio* (whose the rule, his the religion). All these political leaders agreed that a uniform and supreme church was indispensable to a unified kingdom. As James I of England said in 1604, "Where there is no bishop, there is no king." That meant that religious dissent was political dissent, and neither kings nor noblemen (whatever

75

quarrels they might have with each other) were going to put up with it, and particularly not from the common people.

A century of bitter religious and political warfare had torn up the European landscape, particularly the German-speaking regions. Princes and prelates together saw to it that their priests proclaimed and taught the pure approved doctrine of the state, whether Lutheran, Calvinist, or Catholic, nor were they hesitant to hang or to burn whoever seemed to threaten their order.

Order was their overwhelming priority. Faith came to be understood as a rational, dependable definition of order. So the priesthood was trained (trained rather than educated, for the most part) by schooling them in the systematics of a defensive faith. A contemporary participant described early morning lectures on dogmatics:

> [They] filled Anton's head with a good deal of learned lumber, but he learnt how to make divisions and subdivisions, and to go to work systematically. His note books grew bigger and bigger and in less than a year he possessed a complete system, with passages from the Bible to prove it, and a complete polemic against heathen, Turks, Jews, Greeks, Papists, Calvinists. He was able to talk like a book about transubstantiation, the five steps of the exaltation and humiliation of Christ, etc. It was the practice of the Institute where Anton was taught that the adults, who were being educated as schoolmasters, had to distribute themselves among all the churches and take notes on the sermons, which they then submitted to the inspector. Anton now found his pleasure in taking notes of sermons doubled because he saw that in this way he shared the occupation of his teachers.[8]

If in a threatened society the church preached and the state crudely enforced a logical, systematic order, the gospel as good news to ordinary men and women must have to some degree suffered neglect. Nor was the primary source for good news in ready supply. Partly because of the ravages of war, and partly because of the reigning theological spirit, numbers of German parishes during the time of Spener and Francke did not own even one Bible, whether German or Latin. Plowboys equipped with Bibles were at best an unnecessary affliction.

And so things might have continued, except that God has mysterious ways to express his humor. The closed European order was well enough in Luther's time, though we forget at our peril that Columbus's discovery of a new world and Luther's attack on indulgences were separated by only twenty-five years. How could that anxious Saxon monk imagine the effects generated by a pious Genoese sailor who thought he had found the out islands of China, a man whose name Luther probably never heard? A Europe going global was a new thing, as new as the day Julius Caesar brought Rome into Gaul, and then into Britain.

Spener was born the year of Roger Williams's flight to Rhode Island, and the year of the Hooker secession to Connecticut, two events demonstrating the future irrelevancy of the closed European order. The America of "much land, few people" was to be no friend to bishops of any kind, at least not until the continent was safe from kings. But plowboys with energy and some luck were going to do just fine, at least as far as this world measures things. Our evidence is convincing: most commoners in colonial America had nothing to do with religion at all. If this indifference were to be changed, persuasion was the only device—what Roger Williams called "the sword of the spirit." And if this was true of America, it must follow for Europe, even if controlling institutions obscured the facts and obstructed the march to religious freedom during the next two centuries.

America would transform Europe, just as Europe would put its unique stamp on America, chiefly by settlement. But we must not imagine Luther or Calvin, Spener or Francke, Rosenius or Waldenström, sitting down consciously to adapt themselves to an old world being changed by a new world. That is not what they were, or saw, as religious leaders of their day. Martin Buber cautions us about this misunderstanding:

The belief that religious forms arise ever again out of social "relationships" is an error capable of impoverishing the world of the spirit. These relationships influence the sphere within which the forms hold force; only under certain social conditions can the new prepare its way. But the new itself arises from the contacts and conflicts in the heart of religion itself. The economic development supplies here only the fertilizing forces; the spirit supplies the forces of the seed.[9]

The forces of the seed! Here, with Luther, we must tip our hats and pass by in respectful silence. Who except God knows the origin or the destination of "the forces of the seed"? Only after the event do most of us humans know the time of our visitation. Biography tells us something about the driven men and women who founded great movements, but not much about their selection, except that they were usually unlikely candidates for their offices. What search committee will spend much time with a woman or man who stops to hold conversation around burning bushes?

The fathers and mothers of Pietism, Christian and Jewish, were nourished in ancient traditions and committed to them. Their dedication was what made them a problem to office holders; they insisted on holding the tradition to its promises. As Buber says: "Genuine religious movements do not want to offer humans the solution of the world mystery, but to equip them to live from the strength of the mystery; they do not wish to instruct humans about the nature of God, but to show them the path on which they can meet God."[10]

One thinks of Francis of Assisi. This comes naturally for us, for it turns out that extended sections of Arndt's *True Christianity* followed almost word for word the devotionals of a thirteenth-century Franciscan nun named Angela of Foligno.[11] When we think of Spener and Francke, of Winthrop and Wesley, of Rosenius and Nyvall, do we not hear the same language that Buber uses of the founder of Hasidism?

> The Baal-Shem belongs to those central figures of the history of religion whose effect on others has arisen through the fact that they *lived* in a certain way. These men did not proceed *from* a teaching, but moved *to* teaching, in such a way that their life worked as a teaching, as a teaching not yet grasped in words.[12]

And keeping Francke's Halle "foundations" (orphanages, widow homes, schools, Bible printing) fresh in our memory, or, if you prefer, the autonomous growth of nineteeth-century Swedish conventicles, then hear Buber again on what happens when life itself works as a teaching:

> Two things follow. First, that the whole personal attitude of faith that constitutes the essence of this life, works to form community. This does not mean forming a brotherhood, a separated order, removed from public life, which guards an esoteric teaching. It means rather forming community, forming a community of men who remain in families, station, and public ac-

tivity. Within this community, secondly, arise a series of men with the same kind of life, men who have attained a related mode of life in part independently, but first receiving through the master the decisive impulse, the decisive moulding. . . . Each leads an individual life, that, for his part, forms community, therefore a life in the world and with the world, and one that, for its part, again gives birth, in spirit, to men of the same kind.[13]

People of the same kind. Does this mean people of the same class, language, and doctrine? No, rather persons of the same interior posture, the same spiritual experience of the living God, or as John Wesley declared, "If your heart is as my heart, then give me your hand."[14]

The utterly common ground on which Pietists stood together was in their awareness of what had happened to them. Karl Olsson described the Mission Friend unity:

The essence of their togetherness must be understood. The various societies that were formed did not *create* the togetherness of the converts. The revived were bound together by the conversion experience itself. At the very moment when they accepted Christ *personally* they were grafted into the living tree of the *koinonia*. In a moment, in the twinkling of an eye, those who had been afar off were made nigh. . . . The primal fact was the life in Christ and the mystical union of his Body. Their mysticism lay in the consciousness of the presence and comradeship of the Savior among the raw happenings of ordinary life. . . . In his presence they were freed from the shame or tedium of their work; when they plowed or shod horses or tailored or fished, they walked with their King.[15]

Precisely here we find the peculiar genius of historic Pietism. Out of spontaneous joy, its passion is devotion (*devotio*) and service. Francke never tired of saying, "God's glory and neighbor's good."[16] This was all in the context of the larger church, from which he and others of his stamp desired no separation. It is said of Arndt that he

discerned behind the theological conclusions of Luther the function of true doctrine as the perimeter around the experience of penance and salvation; in short, he brought to light again the spontaneity of Christian service as the true fruit of a living faith.

Arndt is entitled to the honor of being the first "Luther scholar" to see, underscore, and apply Luther's vision that justification by faith alone does not preclude but, to the contrary, unleashes good works in terms of the whole Christian, his action in the Church and in the world.[17]

"The perimeter around the experience"—a good phrase. One can have a circle around emptiness; one can also have experiential chaos, an encounter in a hot tub, full of sound and fury and signifying nothing.[18] Neither element by itself satisfied the Pietist fathers and mothers. They wanted both, needed both. Once again, Buber:

> The [movement] may accept the tradition in its present state with undiminished value; its teachings and precepts may be recognized in their full present extension without examining their historical credentials and without comparing them with an original form; but the [movement] creates a new *illumination* of the teachings and precepts, it makes it possible for it to win in this light a new soul, a new meaning, it renews their vitality without changing them in their substance. Here no separation takes place although here too the battle between the old and the new must break out and can take on the most violent forms; the new community remains within the hereditary one and seeks to penetrate it from within—a measuring of two forces against each other, the moving force and the conserving force, a measuring that is soon carried over to the ground of the new community itself and continues among its members, indeed within the heart of each individual.[19]

TRANSPLANTING THE SEED

At first, only Roger Williams argued against an established church in America, contending that the civil order could maintain itself without compelling a religious uniformity. But his was the wave of the continental future. Congregationalism remained the official religion of Massachusetts and Connecticut into the nineteenth century, but the Constitution of 1787 made it clear there would never be a national American church, that religion was a private matter.

What a shock to the children of Rosenius when they first discovered this aspect of the American anthropology! Which of the myriad of American churches was to be their "State Church"? A pioneer pastor during the 1840s in Wisconsin, Gustav Unonius declared for the Episcopalians, on grounds of hierarchical structure. For most Swedes this would not work; they were, after all, Lutheran. The first Swedish pastors—Hasselquist, Carlsson, Andrén—were sympathetic to Rosenius and his programs for low-church reform in Sweden, but came quickly to see that America was a new thing for them. They refused assimilation into broader American Lutheranism, establishing their own Augustana Synod in 1860, and turned steadily toward a more rigid confessionalism.

The great burst of mass migration that immediately following the Civil War brought conventicle Swedes pouring into Chicago, where they tried to repeat exactly their Swedish experience: founding a mission society within the Augustana congregation in 1868, reading from *Pietisten*, and sending out colporteurs. Now came the shock: Augustana ejected them, telling them in effect to rent their own hall and go it on their own! This was America, not Sweden.

Rosenian Swedes, like C. J. Nyvall, did not easily adapt to this new state of affairs. From 1874 to 1875 and again from 1884 to 1885, he visited both the synods of the Mission Friends and the Augustana Synod. He had dear friends in both groups. The death of Rosenius in 1868 (at age fifty-two) and the decision by his widow to give the editorship of *Pietisten* over to Paul Peter Waldenström only weakened old ties. Waldenström's atonement sermon four years later tore up those that remained. This fight between cousins put to an end any hope of a secure Lutheran perimeter for the mission movement, just as the struggle to control the Evangelical National Foundation in Sweden had to lead, at last, to the formation of the Swedish Covenant. But to the end, Waldenström and his friends insisted that the Covenant was not a church but a mission society within the church. He himself had to be badgered to lay aside his ordination in the Church of Sweden.

Seen from the perspective of historic Pietism, the creation of both Covenants (the Swedish in 1878, the American in 1885) can be understood as *devotio* establishing its necessary perimeter. There was no lack of vigor in the *devotio*. Life pulsed inwardly, and the flood of immigrants streamed out over the landscape looking for land to plow and buildings to make. Wherever they went, there also went the mission. The question was how to incarnate the ancient mystical unity, to be faithful to its seed and faithful to the task for which the seed was given. Fred M. Johnson's text for a sermon during the organizational meeting in Chicago in1885 was inspired: "I am a companion of all who fear you, of those who keep your precepts" (Psalm 119:63).

ENDNOTES

1. Gunnar Westin, *George Scott och hans verksamhet i Sverige* (Stockholm: Svenska Kyrans diakonistyrelses bokförlag, 1929), p.622.
2. Ibid.
3. Ibid., p. 631, note 51.
4. See K. James Stein, *Philipp Jakob Spener: Pietist Patriarch* (Chicago: Covenant Press, 1986), pp.93-103 for a summary.
5. See F. Ernest Stoeffler, *The Rise of Evangelical Pietism* (Leiden: E. J. Brill, 1965), *passim*. This is the magisterial work to date on the rise and deployment of world Pietism.
6. Martin Buber, *The Origin and Meaning of Hasidism* (New York: Horizon Press, 1960).
7. Stoeffler, *Rise of Evangelical Pietism*, p. 6. Blaise Pascal was apparently in touch with Jansenist leaders.
8. Karl Philipp Moritz, *Anton Reiser*, tr. P. E. Matheson, *World's Classics* (1926), p.98.
9. Martin Buber, *Hasidism*, p. 62.
10. Ibid., p. 115.
11. Johan Arndt, *True Christianity*, Peter Erb, ed. and trans. (New York: Paulist Press, 1979), pp.10—12.
12. Buber, *Hasidism*, p. 25.
13. Ibid.
14. Quoted in Stoeffler, *Rise of Evangelical Pietism*, p.7.
15. Karl A. Olsson, *By One Spirit* (Chicago: Covenant Publications, 1962), p. 214.
16. Gary R. Sattler, *God's Glory, Neighbor's Good*, (Chicago: Covenant Press, 1982).
17. Peter Erb in Arndt, *True Christianity*, p. xv.
18. See Thomas C. Oden, *The Intensive Group Experience: The New Pietism* (Philadelphia: Westminster Press, 1972), *passim*, for a critique of the secular encounter group movement.
19. Martin Buber, *Hasidism*, p.114.

CHAPTER 7

The Covenant: Being

Midwinter Conference Address, February 7, 1985
Chicago, Illinois

W hen all things began, the Word already was. The Word dwelt with God, and what God was, the Word was. The Word, then, was with God at the beginning, and through him all things came to be; no single thing was created without him. All that came to be was alive with his life, and that life was the light of men. The light shines on in the dark, and the darkness has never mastered it.

John 1:1-5, The New English Bible

We who are gathered here this morning are, ourselves, individually and corporately, the living evidences of the creative power of the Word. At the moment of our conception, four small words in our genes, about a millionth of the length of the DNA chain (A for adenine, G for guanine, C for cytosine, and T for thymine) begin sending signals to the more than twenty kinds of amino acids from which very complex proteins will be assembled out of the jumble of nutrients in the womb.

Fetal growth is explosive: from a barely visible egg to a fully articulated six or seven pound infant in nine months. But more astonishing still is the power of the original word to control and define the staggering complexity of the fetus, saying to some cells, "You shall be bone," to others, "You shall be flesh," and to still others, "You shall be brain."

Aristotle observed this process at the macroscopic level, speculating that in every species the growth of the individual fetus recapitulates the evolutionary history of the species. I understand that this cliché is no longer popular among cell biologists. But the psalmist grasped the core of a very modern viewpoint in his hymn (Psalm 139: 13-18):

Thou it was who didst fashion my inward parts;
thou didst knit me together in my mother's womb.

83

I will praise thee, for thou dost fill me with awe;
wonderful thou art, and wonderful thy works.
Thou knowest me through and through:
my body is no mystery to thee,
how I was secretly kneaded into shape
and patterned in the depths of the earth.
Thou didst see my limbs unformed in the womb,
and in thy book are they all I recorded;
day by day they were fashioned,
not one of them was late in growing.
How deep I find thy thoughts, O God,
how inexhaustible their themes!
Can I count them? They outnumber the grains of sand;
to finish the count, my years must equal thine.

Through our lives, from conception to death, this intense conversation between the word and the flesh it has created goes on. The word, buried deep in the quiet center of our innermost definitive cells, and the flesh, subject to the blessings and outrages of the surrounding world, send back and forth via complex messenger systems an unending stream of information: "I am hurt, I need repair," "I am puzzled, put someone to work on this problem," "I am hungry, send food."

There was a time when others urged us to believe that we are simply blank slates, waiting for the surrounding environment to shape our destinies. And it is indeed the case that we do not escape, ever in our lives, the world around us. It is to live in this world that the flesh has been formed, as the Greeks used to say, out of earth and air, fire and water, or as we might prefer today, out of stored sunlight.

There was a time when others urged us to believe that all is tending to entropy, that undifferentiated chaos toward which the second law of thermodynamics points. As heat cannot flow uphill, but must always flow toward the colder, so must all things degrade themselves. And, indeed, we live daily with the experience of degradation, as Robert Frost reminds us in "Mending Wall": "Something there is that doesn't love a wall,/that wants it down." Our lives do seem, sometimes, to be an unremitting struggle against things that fall apart. Our shoulders ache with the struggle to hold things together.

There was a time when others urged us to believe that all things are determined, a cosmic machine set in motion by a distant God for his own amusement, a clockwork mechanism grinding out its mindless predictabilities according to the formulae of Isaac Newton, of whom the poet sang, "Newton alone gazed on Nature bare." And indeed, we do find, on the macroscopic scale, a wonderful, if somewhat more complicated regularity than the sainted Newton visualized. Even Einstein could reflect that God might be mysterious, but never tricky.

And there was a time when others urged us to believe that all things are changing by accident. Chance mutation, validated by success in the struggle to survive, and thus transmitted to the next generation, which in turn survives because of its superior equipment, is the root secret of life. And, indeed, we cannot doubt any longer the existence of genetic mutation, for we bring it about, not exactly by chance, in laboratories and in a global atmosphere poisoned by chemicals and radioactivity we have ourselves released.

But when Alfred Russell Wallace, the young naturalist who was Darwin's chief rival for the honor of having discovered the principle of natural selection, wrote to Darwin to express his theoretical doubts, because he thought that the human brain was a most astonishingly excessive organ if mere survival were the end purpose of evolution, Darwin curtly replied that he did not wish to discuss the matter. For reasons best known to himself and his successors (and perhaps partly because of the uninformed and contemptuous nature of his public opposition) Darwin preferred his solipsism about accident to any hypothesis about evolution that involved conscious purpose, or as old-fashioned people might have said, Providence: "How deep I find thy thoughts, O God, how inexhaustible their themes!"

I stand in my classroom, waiting to read the class roll. I look at the new class. And there I see a turn of the head, a way of carrying the shoulders, a glint in the eye that takes me, in memory, a generation back in time. This is the child of my former student, well-remembered by some miracle of the brain; I am not surprised when the new one answers to the old name. But I am continually surprised, as the term goes on, by the new. So similar in some respects, so different in others, in some cases at least so refreshingly different. Says the psalmist: "[Thy themes] outnumber the grains of sand; to finish the count, my years must equal thine."

Inescapably but marvelously, we are creatures. In each of us there is a deep structure that transcends all time and space, a givenness that reflects faithfully the Word that made us, and continues daily to make us. We are, each of us individually, reflections of the sovereignty of the original Word. As the Word became flesh in Jesus Christ, and dwelt among us, in glory and majesty incomparable, so even we, imperfect as we are, reflect that same mysterious process of incarnation. If this be true, we are in a deep sense the enfleshed messages of the Word.

So it is as well in this fellowship we share: this Covenant, these thousands of people, these hundreds of congregations, these institutions, this living web of relationships, visible and invisible. All that the Covenant has been, is today, and will be tomorrow, begins and lives on under the sovereign impulse of the Word.

First, is the Incarnate Word, the living Christ who came striding over the stormy waters of their disrupted lives to our fathers and mothers in the faith, bringing that healing, that meaning, that liberation we call salvation. The same living Christ whose coming to us has made us alive to serve, the same living Christ who will come to generations unborn, until the Father's loving work is completed and all is made ready for the final celebration.

Second, is the Inspired Word, the endlessly rich, the endlessly sufficient well from which thirsty creatures draw image, acquaintance, metaphor, story, instruction. This is the Bible, the whole Word of God, suffused so mysteriously with the presence of the Holy Spirit that believers and unbelievers alike testify to its power.

Beside Jesus and the Bible, I add a third word, hoping to be understood: the Word which we are, as persons, both in our creation and in our recreation. Imperfect as we are, we are yet, in ourselves, messages from God to each other, in that incarnated form we creatures most readily understand. The Word who created us, the Word who saves us, the Word who inspires and instructs us is also the Word of that great cloud of witnesses that intersects our lives both in recollection and in our daily work.

Who would we be without the saints of God? In what darkness might we have sat, but for the light they have reflected for us? In what meaningless chaos of "sound and fury, signifying nothing," might we have been lost, but for their reassuring touch? In what gray and cheerless hell might we be wandering, had not one of these put us on the bus to heaven? The list of those to whom I owe any life worth having is long; it begins with Abraham and includes not a few sitting in this room today.

I say this not to wring a sentimental tear from you this morning, but to emphasize the meaning and dignity of our human participation in the work of the Word. A man told me once that he needed a new overcoat badly, and saved to buy it. But he saw that his sister needed a coat also, so he used the money to buy one for her. "Praise the Lord," said she, "He knew I needed a coat." The man said to me, with a hurt look, "Why couldn't she at least have said thanks to me?" Why indeed? An ungracious spirit may wear Christian dress as easily as any other, and never more righteously than when badged with a few slogans and a handful of abstractions. But for us it really is as Robert Frost says in "Kitty Hawk": "The supreme merit lay in risking spirit in substantiation." And that is not only a Yankee poet's brief paraphrase of John 1, but a kind of capsule statement of our Covenant experience of the centrality of incarnation.

The true genius of the Pietism that Spener and Francke practiced, the conventicle movement that in spontaneous ways grew up from the 1850s and on in Sweden, lay at the intersection of the Word with the daily experience of small groups of quite ordinary people, who hungered and thirsted for meaning in a world coming apart before their eyes. The disorders afflicting them were profound: a world was breaking up, a new one appearing full of disjointed strangenesses. Peasant villages as old as medieval Europe were disappearing, replaced by modern farms. Population was growing too quickly to be sustained by the old rural order, and jobs in new industries were still too few. The ancient isolation was pierced by new messages, chiefly the word about America, the Promised Land, California gold, and Lincoln's 1862 Homestead Act. First in a trickle, then in a stream, then in a flood (like the Irish and the Germans before them), Swedes packed up their little sea chests and sailed for America—more than one million of them, before it was over, one million out of five million, 20 percent of the Swedish people.

We cannot understand fully the meaning of that vast European migration of which this was a part, and of the accelerating rates of social change that are partly its consequence and continue to unsettle people today. We have learned much, however, and we may be quite sure that an ordinary Swede understood even less than we, armed as we are with hindsight, and standing at a later stage in this global process. All they knew was that the earth was shaking under their feet. A lot of them responded in the time-honored Scandinavian way: they got royally drunk on potato brandy. Others toughed it out in stolid routines, living from day to day as they could, without any particular sense of direction. Still others, and in growing numbers, joined the local conventicle, and there became *läsare* (readers).

See them, this handful of ordinary people, few with any formal education to speak of, but most of them at least literate, thanks chiefly to their catechetical instruction. Peasants, tailors, cobblers, iron-mongers and blacksmiths, hired hands and servant girls. See them gathered, illegally by the way (before 1858), in their small circles, reading with each other—reading Luther, yes; reading Carl Olof Rosenius's *Pietisten*, yes; reading Peter Fiellstedt's *Mission News*, yes. But above all, reading the Bible, verse by verse, chapter by chapter, book by book, again and again and again during a whole generation, until they had got it in them like bone of their bone, flesh of their flesh.

Occasionally, they had visits from colporteurs like the young Carl Johan Nyvall, or from itinerating lay preachers like Horse-August Anderson, or from young theological students like Paul Peter Waldenström, or even from the great Rosenius himself. But the conventicle had its own local life, its own unanswerable autonomy in the familiar circle. Waldenström remembered coming to one peasant cabin where the circle was so crowded and the smoke of peasant pipes so intense that as he spoke he watched with fascination as the candles went out one by one for lack of oxygen. Armed with deep biblical acquaintance, and sharing familiar experience over time, the conventicles could reach out in their own localities with realism.

As the conventicles grew, they reached out to each other, forming mission societies, even provincial associations. But the growth of the folk remained familiar. If they could not yet give themselves a name, they knew with precision who they were within themselves and with each other. When the theological and organizational storm clouds finally burst, pouring down controversy and confusion, people readily sorted themselves out pretty much according to a generation of experience. What was more natural than that the people of the conventicles should cry, "Where is it written?" They knew precisely where to look. And as for those who had already responded to the siren call of America, their first act in Chicago or Galesburg or Princeton or Swede Bend was to try to reproduce, as faithfully as they could, the family of faith they had left behind them. They knew each other immediately. They had a lot to learn about the American scene, but they knew each other from an older Swedish experience.

It is well that we remember how unlikely all this really was. When in the late 1840s Carl Johan Nyvall's mother began to sit with Olof Olsson's mother to read the Bible together, encouraged by their young assistant parish priest, neither of them imagined Lindsborg, Kansas, or Chicago, Illinois. They thirsted for the water of life with a kind of dim intuition that it could be had, and sent their buckets into the well. Everything else followed, in wave after wave of increasingly complex structure.

There is a cosmic arrow pointing irreversibly toward entropy, toward a final equilibrium of all things in which there are no structures and therefore no information, only noise. We have managed to get this second law of thermodynamics into our souls; it is part of the air we breathe, and responsible, I think, for our grim workaholic struggle against the very elements of the cosmos. Please remember that the physics that underpin our common-sense understandings today were mostly formed during the nineteenth century when railroads, coal, and steel were the great objects of social progress, and heat transfer efficiencies meant dollars and cents.

There is another arrow, the arrow of history, and it points not to entropy but to creation, to structures of ever increasing versatility and complexity. These structures are packed with information and alive with surprise. That the cosmos is intricately connected, unbelievably web-like, we can understand in the estimation that the microscopic state of a gas in a laboratory would be altered significantly in a fraction of a second if a single gram of matter as far away as Sirius, the dog star, were to be moved a distance of only one centimeter. It follows that mortals like us are at a loss to predict the course of such intricately related events. Only let me remind you again of the psalmist's trembling recognition: "[Your themes] outnumber the grains of sand; to finish the count, my years must equal thine."

I tip my hat, then, with Luther, and pass by this passion for prediction and control, for the years of my life are three score years and ten, perhaps. But something in the vagrant breeze I sniff says that the Word is at work, building, building, ceaselessly active, vital, creative, and surprising! It is a grave mercy, after all, this sovereignty of the Word, this total independence of my control. How else could I sleep at night? So Nils Frykman could sing:

> Why should I be anxious? I have such a Friend,
> Who bears in his heart all my woe;
> This friend is the Savior, on him I depend,
> His love is eternal, I know.
> (*The Covenant Hymnal*, #431)

That man was a schoolteacher, a good one, deprived of his job because he was a Reader. Forced, in effect, to emigrate, he found a home high on the hill at Salem, Kandiyohi County, Minnesota. He sang like the nightingale, and gave wise counsel to young David Nyvall about the running of Skogsbergh's school, in a fine, neat hand.

My dear sisters and brothers in this beloved Covenant, what is it, at last, that I mean to say to you? I know you well. You have given faithful service, almost always beyond any reasonable estimate of duty, and the majority of you, at levels of economic support not likely to enrich your golden years. Yet you serve the daily work, faithful to your calling, knowing your sheep by name. Our faith and our history bring us one clear message, one clear note from the silent deeps: Trust the Word! Trust the Word!

First, trust the Word, which we are for ourselves and for each other. What a Babel of noise we live in today. The sheer scale of the billions of people on our planet suggests the insignificance of persons, and this is reinforced by the daily abrasion inflicted on us by the media and by the fractionating demands of a culture of specialization. Human personality suffers overload, the worst part of it the inward uncertainty of identity.

How strangely comforting it is to have the full attention, the comradeship, of a dimensional human being, a fully grown person with virtues and faults, but with a coherence about him or her visible from all angles, and without the guile of projected images. The proof of this lies in the stories we tell each other. Are they not about the angularities of real people?

To have faith in the Word that we are is in one sense what the Covenant pioneers called "the one thing needful," the surprising and joy-bringing experience of salvation from meaninglessness:

O let your soul now be filled with gladness,
Your heart redeemed, rejoice indeed!
O may the thought banish all your sadness
That in his blood you have been freed,
That God's unfailing love is yours,
That you the only Son were given,
That by his death he has opened heaven,
That you are ransomed as you are.
(*The Covenant Hymnal*, #494)

That you are ransomed *as you are*. We have, praise God, the right to be ourselves. He who attacks our selves attacks the Word of God, and among the attackers not least is that unreconstructed part of ourselves that persists in doubting God's wisdom in making us as we are. I know my faults, my need for amendment in this or that respect. But improvement can only proceed from a firm center a confidence, an assurance that comes from an authority unquestionable.

Trust the Word, which you are. It is the deep center of your pastoral authority or whatever your vocation might be, your own authentic style. As God looked upon his work of creation and called it good, so you must be able to judge your own work with assurance. If you must wait for the applause or are reticent for fear of criticism, the church will be driven by every whimsical wind until at last even the truth disappears.

Trust the Word, then, which you are for each other, and for us all. A fellowship is a structure built out of a Word, requiring that same ceaseless cybernetic flow of messages, of information, for its health. I emphasize cybernetic (feedback) because one-way information is a dead end. It is a broken circuit, a balloon filling and filling with gas until at last it must burst. Just as in our own bodies the messenger circuits must ceaselessly inform the cell makers what is going on so that repairs may be made, so in our fellowship we must not allow ourselves to be distracted from this necessity to speak and to listen. Nor is this a word especially directed to Covenant Offices in Chicago, for information in a complex body must flow within the parts as well as between the parts and the agencies of direction. If I have a fear for our Covenant future today, it lies in a feeling that we may tend to undervalue the Word, which we are for each other, or, at least, to allow the connections between us to decay.

My own studies in the yellowing pages of the pioneer newspapers and periodicals have surprised me again and again with the speed and amplitude of the information they dispensed, with the wonderfully personal quality of the materials, with the sense of timely engagement they afforded to the fellowship. One had a constant flow of *news* from people and places near and far, and one had it weekly. It was possible for correspondents to read and reply in the next issue—not always in an edifying way, perhaps, but surely it was lively.

My brother, the editor, will forgive me, I know, if I speak of *The Covenant Companion* without his prior permission. I like it, and I read it, cover to cover. But it is too small and it arrives too seldom to bear the weight of the shared information our Covenant fellowship needs for the rich and multilateral awarenesses that feed a face-to-face fellowship like ours. And even then, there are congregations that declare they can no longer afford it, at an annual cost per person of one inexpensive dinner out.

Perhaps something else is at work here that needs our thoughtful attention. I have the impression that congregations, and the needs of congregations, are increasingly becoming our priority unit of account at the expense of our comprehensive sense of the church. Some of this is due, no doubt, to the recent push for church growth. There are now local congregations in which there has been no time for assimilation to the Covenant family, in which neither pastor nor laity see any compelling reason to look beyond purely local concerns. That there are purely local concerns, I do not doubt. We must not, however, neglect our own orderly housekeeping. But there is a kind of congregational narcissism that denies the larger fellowship in the name of local concern, and ends by impoverishing itself by reason of limited vision, as all self-preoccupation does.

Coming as they did to a vast landscape, themselves so few, the pioneers did quite naturally what we perhaps must learn again to do. They traveled to each other and to each other's people, preaching and discussing, praying and singing, sleeping on the parlor room floor if necessary. The mission meetings (Nyvall called them folk-universities on wheels) were instruments of the larger fellowship where non-stop preaching and discussion united pastors and laity, a vital and jovial experience garnished with mountains of food and baptized with gallons of coffee.

How I miss the grand gatherings of my boyhood. The thousands of the Cook County Young People, of Chatauqua, of Mission Springs, even of the Saturday night Mission League basketball games. How I prayed, all week, that my Austin heroes would triumph gloriously over those scoundrels from Grand Crossing. And how conscious I was, therefore, that there *was* a Grand Crossing, and that it was Covenant. What a visibility, what a human visibility that fellowship was for me, growing up.

My brothers and sisters, we must travel to each other. We are, in ourselves, in our own flesh, the best and most reliable information about the fellowship. I know from my own experience, often repeated, that I return from meeting you inspired and refreshed, because, as Hopkins sings, "The Holy Ghost broods o'er the bent earth with warm breath, and, ah! bright wings." Trust the Word!

Second, trust the Word, which is the whole Word of God. We take food daily. It is the raw material from which the Word in us fashions our daily renewal. The laws of the flesh are reliable and insistent about this. We must eat, or else we die. For this fellowship, the need for Bible is equally insistent. The Bible is our food, our nourishment, the meat and drink of our identity. Listen to a part of David Nyvall's hymn to the New Testament in his essay on "Covenant Ideals":

> The value of the New Testament, considered as our constitution, is pastoral. It is the voice of the Shepherd. We claim to possess in the New Testament a constitution that is unparalleled, if what we desire is not only a condition for living in peace with our neighbors in the manner of comity and federation, but the only tested and approved condition for organized unity, including all the followers of Christ on local, national and international lines. . . . Creeds speak dialects, often archaic beyond the possibility of translation. Faith speaks the universal language of want, the original tongue in which the human heart and Christ converse.[1]

And again:

> The New Testament is not a dream book, but like all real life has the stuff of which dreams are made. Without being a confession, and just because of that fact, the New Testament excels all written confessions by the number of truths expressed and implied, by the absence of errors, and by the fact that what-

ever truth it has in common with any confession is more simply and more clearly expressed in the New Testament.[2]

We have been, and are today of absolute necessity, a people of the Book. It feeds us, it inspires us, it constrains us, it disciplines us, it challenges us. Living in it, we are secure, hearing the voice of the Shepherd. Wandering from it, we go astray, nibbling our way like dumb sheep into far canyons and rocky places. Is it then our assimilation to Canaan, our affluence, our intellectual and social sophistication that masks our true hunger for the Bread of Life? Bread is bread for us only on the condition that we eat it. Or is it that the Bible requires being read, and in our age, reading seems to have fallen on bad times? I have a dear colleague, a poet, who complains of the difficulty of composing poems for people who cannot understand allusion, who do not have the information to understand metaphor.

It is strange to hear people speaking of defending the Bible. God help us all if the Bible needs our defense. I find lay people of extraordinary training and intelligence whose grasp of the wholeness of the Bible is childish and jittery. All they have is a smattering of verses, strung up like beads on a string, and a set of opinions about them that will hardly bear mature examination. Can we set a more important priority for ourselves than to plunge ourselves wholeheartedly back into that life-giving stream? Whatever else we may mean by Christian education we must mean instruction in Bible, the whole Bible. Trust the Word!

Finally, trust the Word himself, Jesus Christ the Lord. All, all is of him. Permit me to quote David Nyvall once more:

> If I have found Christ by the testimony of this book, the book entices me to find him in every richer and fuller meanings. And when I have once found him completely, as he found me, so that I no longer see through a glass dimly, but face to face in full clarity, then I have lived through what Peter means when he encourages us to give attention to the prophetic word as to a lamp shining in a dark place, *until the day dawns and the light shines in our hearts.* When full days comes, the torches which guided us through the night go out. Until this, the Bible remains; Christ remains beyond this. One did not read the Bible in paradise; there, life itself was the light. Therefore the Bible

cannot now replace Christ, who is the light, yes, the way, both truth and life.

Only one word remains for me to say: to express, to you all, representing this beloved fellowship in the richness of its past, in the vitality and promise of its present and its future, my endless gratitude that you have allowed me membership here. My father used to say, with deep emotion: "All I have, I owe to the Covenant. All I am belongs to it." And so by the grace of God, say I.

ENDNOTES

1. David Nyvall, "Covenant Ideals," in Glenn P. Anderson, ed., *Covenant Roots: Sources and Affirmations* (Chicago: Covenant Publications, 1999), p. 160

2. Ibid., p. 158.

CHAPTER 8

God's Glory, Neighbor's Good

Covenant Founders' Day Address, February 20, 1994
New Brighton, Minnesota

O
*h, give thanks to the Lord, for he is good; for his steadfast love
endures forever. Let the redeemed of the Lord say so, those
redeemed from trouble and gathered in from the lands, from the
east and from the west, from the north and from the south.*

Psalm 107:1-3

My dear brothers and sisters in Christ:

We have it from the Apostle Paul that we are clay pots. But
we are clay pots filled with treasure from God. And in the quietness of
this hour, I should like you fellow clay pots to reflect with some imagination about the treasure you contain.

First of all, the treasure of Christ, Jesus the Savior and Jesus the
Lord; the grace of God; the treasure of memory; and, for those of you
who tonight have eyes to see, that host of white-robed witnesses ringing
us in this room, asking if we mean to carry on their Covenant work—
people from East and West and from North and South, gathered.

Think tonight how strange and mysterious it is that each of us is
here. Most of us have come from far places, and our coming here is a series of mysterious incidents, none of which were clear when they were
occurring. As my colleague and friend Mel Soneson loves to say, "God
works best in the midst of chaos." While we much prefer the settled
order, God stirs his great finger in history and sends his unwilling servants out into the desert where, of all places, they do not want to go.
Why would a nice Swedish girl from Småland end up in Minneapolis?
Why would a nice Swedish boy from Värmland end up in Chicago of all
places? And why would any Swede at all end up in Kansas?

We are here, as a people and as persons, as the consequence of a vast movement in human history—a movement that uprooted millions and millions of European people out of their accustomed native soil and projected them out into a new land of promise. It is not a mistake that one of our own metaphors for our institutional experience is the ancient metaphor of Israel leaving Egypt, searching for the Promised Land. So, tonight we feel, I hope, our sense of connection with the mystery of those beginnings, which then implies our own sense of connection with the mystery of our continuing life. For, as one African American preacher asked former president Milton Engebretsen in a very direct way at an Annual Meeting or a Midwinter Conference some years ago: "Now, Milt, you've got all these nice people here in the United States of America. What do you intend to do with them?" I am not aware that there was an answer that night, but it is our question tonight.

Is there anyone else in this assemblage tonight as astonished as I am that it is already nine years since the centennial celebration, which I think most of you remember—with pleasure. Nine years! Or is it just my advancing age that says the time is telescoping? One hundred and nine years ago on a terribly snowy day in the city of Chicago, in the balcony of the old Tabernacle at 30th and LaSalle, about sixty-five men sat together and concluded that there was a possibility of binding themselves to each other. This came after a long and bitter discussion, and troublesome mutual experience. But, it was finally arrived at on the basis of F. M. Johnson's keynote sermon to the assembled delegates, based on Psalm 119:63: "I am a companion of all who fear you, of those who keep your precepts." I am a companion of all who fear you.

What they were groping for, these green immigrants, was a satisfying and effective relationship that would express authentically their own devotional and theological experience, both back home in Sweden and here in this strange new land. They wanted a principle of order that was a guarantee of the freedom, of the joy they already had experienced in the gospel. They did not want to sacrifice either order or freedom, but they were living within sight of the Tower of Babel.

Several thousand "Amelikites" arrived daily in Chicago during the late nineteenth century, that exploding town where the prairie met Lake Michigan. Amelikites—people of a thousand different tongues and traditions, as threatening to this little group of Swedes as ever were the

Amelikites to the children of Moses. What would be their principle of order? What would be their security here in this strange land where everyone called them dumb Swedes? What would be, after all, the possibility of accomplishing a secure sense of identity in a place as confusing as Chicago was?

Finally, they were driven by their own experience. It was an experience of forty years of cell-going, conventicle-sharing, of devotions, and finally at the rock, the experience of God's grace—his own ineffable grace in their lives. That primal experience, however it is received, in whatever style and in whatever time span, bound these people together with a network of meaning. The primal experience, the experience of grace.

On a Sunday in 1687, a young German theological student named August Hermann Francke found himself in profound spiritual anguish. He later recorded his experiences:

> I intended to go to bed as in earlier unrest, and decided that if I experienced no change I would again refuse to preach, for I could not preach in unbelief and against my own heart and thus deceive the people. I also did not know whether it would be possible for me because I felt much too deeply what it was to have no God on whom one's heart can rest, bemoaning one's sins and not knowing why or who he is who presses out such tears or whether there is truly a God who is angered thereby; to one's sorrow and great distress daily and yet know no Savior nor refuge. In such great anxiety I fell again to my knees on that Sunday eve and cried to God—whom I neither knew nor believed—for salvation from such a sorrowful condition, if there was truly a God. Then the Lord heard me, the living God from his holy throne, as I was still on my knees. So great was his fatherly love that he would not take away such doubt and restlessness of heart little by little—with which I would have been quite content, but rather he suddenly heard me so that I would be all the more convinced and would bridle my strayed reason to use nothing against his power and faithfulness. Then, as one turns his hand (in a twinkling), so all my doubts were gone; I was sure in my heart of the grace of God in Christ Jesus; I knew God not only as God but rather as one called my Father. All

sadness and unrest in my heart was taken away in a moment. On the contrary, I was suddenly so overwhelmed with such a stream of joy that I praised out of high spirits the God who had shown me such great grace. I rose again of a completely different mind than when I had knelt down. I bent down with great sorrow and doubt, but arose again with inexpressible joy and great assurance. As I knelt, I did not believe there was a God. As I arose, I would have confirmed it without fear or doubt, even with the shedding of my blood.[1]

Those things happen. Sometimes silently, sometimes with little more than a sigh, sometimes with the shaking as of volcanoes—but those things happen. That mysterious grace occurs. And the memory of it transforms life. That is what it is to be gathered in. To be gathered in, and then to be sent out. This same young August Hermann Francke spent six months with the founder of German Pietism, Philipp Jakob Spener. Spener became his mentor, and he sent Franke first up to Hamburg to work. To work with whom? To work, in the peculiar way that Pietists always seem to have worked, with children. He found the lost deserted kids in the teeming city of Hamburg and learned how to teach them.

And then, on Spener's recommendation, Francke was sent to the new university at Halle, where he was given the chair in Greek and Hebrew and, to eke out his income, the pastoral charge of a noxious suburb of Halle, the little burg of Glaucha. Very quickly he began to work with the children of Glaucha. First, finding in the almsbox of his church a sum the equivalent of seventy dollars, he resolved, on that basis, to take it as a signal from God to establish a school in his home. And he began. And very soon, the reputation of the school spread until there were middle class and nobles trying to get their children into his school because he was running the best school in the district. That being not enough, he established a free lunch for penniless students at the University of Halle, so at least they got one square meal a day. From the school, he established orphanages, several of them; and then a home for widows; and, finally, in cooperation with Baron von Canstein of Berlin, he formed the Canstein Press, which took it as its charter to print inexpensive Bibles for distribution all over Germany. Within a hundred years, the press had printed 1,200,000 Bibles in a country, which, ravaged by post-Reformation religious warfare, had many parishes that had not seen a Bible for a generation.

These were the famous Halle Foundations. And they illustrate the double-sided proposition that Pietism brought into the modem world. First, *God's glory*, this inexpressible sense of the glory, the majesty, and the grace of God, without which the soul simply cannot live. This sense, sometimes acute in us, sometimes moribund in us, but once in, always there. God's glory. And, because of God's glory and as a conclusion from it, *neighbor's good*. Not as a separate matter, but as integral with the glory of God. Because of this, I am mobilized and active according to my neighbor's need. In accord with Jesus's own commandment, you will recall in Matthew 22:37-40, the first and greatest commandment and the second commandment. On these two commandments, says Jesus himself, hang all the law and the prophets.

The foundations at Halle achieved a global reputation. And it was in that same spirit that John Wesley of the Church of England, having been influenced by German Moravian missionaries to Georgia, found his heart strangely warmed at Aldersgate, eleven years after the death of Francke. As someone once said, tongue in cheek, Wesley did not leave much of a legacy—a set of spoons and the Methodist Church. And also in his legacy was a young Wesleyan pastor named George Scott, who came to Sweden at the invitation of an industrialist, who established the first machine tool factory in Sweden, to preach to his English workers. Scott soon learned to speak Swedish and enrolled in his wider efforts a young Swedish Lutheran named Carl Olaf Rosenius. When Scott had to leave the country, for reasons of Swedish hostility, Rosenius remained behind to edit the newspaper that Scott had begun, *Pietisten*.

And so it was with Maria Nilsdotter, a widow living in Värmland outside Karlskoga—bitter and hopeless, restless and unhappy, with six children and no future. She had attended her parish church in Karlskoga, and from the pastor of that parish church she heard *ortho doxy*, that is, a demand for unreasoning obedience and, above all, a demand of a young peasant widow that she make no waves and ask no questions. Life out there in the woods was dark. She was, as Francke had said two hundred years earlier, without the hope of a savior, full of sorrow, until a young assistant pastor in that parish put her in touch with another woman of the same mind, Britta Jonsdotter. He suggested that the two sit down to begin to read Luther's *Postila* (sermons), and the Bible together. They read for several years, and gradually accumulated along with them, in that same parish, other women. Until, little by little (as my old colleague at North Park, Bill Fredrickson, used to say, "You can't read Bible very long without running into Jesus"), Maria came to the conclusion that God's grace was real and that it was for her—in her own way—this primal experience.

And suddenly she began making a pest of herself all over the parish—delivering seditious (meaning mission-minded) newspapers, in general upsetting people's apple carts by insisting on enlarging the local conventicle, and, finally, just as Francke did, coming from God's glory to neighbor's good. How? She went and found children who were lost. She brought them to her farm—this is a widow with six children, now—brought them to her farm with no visible means of support and began to teach them Sunday-school style, which meant not only religious instruction but also reading, writing, ciphering, and the other things a kid needs as a foundation for education.

She discovered that having had them only on Sunday, they were soon uproarious the rest of the week. And let me tell you, people in those neighborhoods lived a raw life. So she thought, "I've got to have these kids with me all week if they're to have any chance." She went to the county Poor Relief Board and asked that the children be placed on her farm as at an orphanage. They refused. She was a troublemaker, she was a Pietist, she was a member of the conventicle, she was an unreliable female, and she did not know her place. So, she talked with the other women in the conventicle, and then went where they auctioned these children off and bought them, brought them back to the orphanage, clothed and fed them, dressed and taught them, though she had no educational degree or certification, and gave them a chance at a full life. God's glory, neighbor's good.

This woman then pressed her son, Carl Johan, into the service of the gospel when his primal experience came. And in due time, he became something like the Free Church bishop of all of Värmland and was an essential architect of the Covenant in Sweden. He was in that balcony on February 20, 1885, with his Swedish-American brethren when the American Covenant was formed. And his son, Maria's grandson, was David Nyvall, founding president of North Park. Britta's son was Olof Olsson, the founding Augustana pastor of the settlement in Lindsborg, Kansas, and later president of Augustana College in Rock

Island, Illinois. Two women living out the gospel. God's glory, neighbor's good.

This is what made Maria's grandson David write: "With us as with the Apostolic Church, strength lies not in number and accomplishments, nor in order and discipline, nor even in health and wealth; our outlook is certainly not in any telescopic vision of the immensity of nature nor in any microscopic vision of its depth, but in the constitutional sufficiency of faith."[2] *The constitutional sufficiency of faith.*

Are you troubled tonight, my friends, that we are comparatively so small? Do you long to be a member of a church of 32,000,000? Would it make you happy to have everybody quite clear that we are not the Convent Church, but the Covenant Church? You see, the genius of the discovery of the grace of God is that it is entirely suited to the person to whom it is given—and to that person alone. That is how we have our names with each other. And out of the work we do with each other, we have the habits of the heart by which we become truly, to use the Swedish, *förbundet* (Covenant), meaning bound together. Or to take that secular word and give it its permanent Judeo-Christian weight, this is how we became covenanted together in mission and, to use the language of my boyhood, became Mission Friends.

Do you remember when we were Mission Friends? Not just friends in mission, but members of the mission who were, as members of the mission, friends. And friends because we were of the mission. And the mission—not simply separated congregations—but the mission wherever there were Mission Friends who had God's glory and neighbor's good to see to. No barriers between the congregations, no artificial sense that I belong to this and I belong to that. Mission Friends. So that, whether I visit here with you in Salem or am in my church at North Park in Chicago, I can, as a Mission Friend, help to plant trees with the Carlson Foundation in Zaire. I can help with Covenant Pines Bible Camp in MacGregor, Minnesota. I can help at Unalakleet. I can help at Swedish Covenant Hospital.

In fact, one year after they founded the Covenant Church, Henry Palmblad, director of the City Mission Society in Chicago, went around and put the finger on all the Mission Friends he could locate on the street and said, "You know what we need? We need, here, a home of mercy." Why? Because people were being lost and hurt and damaged in the violence of the migration. There had to be a place to care for people.

So Palmblad mustered the first Covenant president. Carl August Björk— a great big ex-cobbler of a man whom nobody turned down if they wanted to remain spiritually healthy—who kept a little notebook in his pocket in which he wrote down what he expected of each person and what he got. And they bought a farm at Bowmanville and established the Home of Mercy. Neighbor's good. These Mission Friends understood the primal glory of God. Their next mission was to take over the Swedish Covenant's mission in Alaska, at a place called Unalakleet. We are still there. There was no distinction between local and foreign. Mission wherever there is neighbor's good.

Well, I have no more time. That's been my history as a history teacher, by the way. In fact, I said in later years that history was accumulating faster than I could teach it. I want to say, however, one more word. It would be a mistake tonight to imagine that these people, upon whom God's benediction rests, were better people than we are—were more pious, had fewer struggles, or felt less despair. And with that in mind, I want to read to you a letter from L. J. Peterson of Princeton, Illinois, dated 1871, printed in an early Covenant newspaper.

> Finally, brothers and sisters, oh, only a short time and then an eternal rest, an eternal year of peace which will never be interrupted by outward crosses or by inward vexation. Instead we will always be together with our Jesus and undisturbed enjoy his holy fellowship. May God, from whom all grace comes, fill our dead, cold, lukewarm, empty, narrow, sluggish, careless, false, hypocritical, unfaithful, doubting, frivolous, erring, godless, corrupted, dispirited, depressed, sorrowful, *glad* hearts, often without peace, with the comfort of peace and faith and keep us through evil or good reputation, through darkness and light, to happily come home to our dear Lord, that we see him eternally as he is, face to face.[3]

Brothers, sisters, we have had an eternally blessed meeting. We have been called out of darkness and gathered into *förbundet*, into covenant, by God for mission, for God's glory, and for neighbor's good. May God richly bless the Covenant Church, not because it is big, not because it is important in the eyes of the world, but because it is the authentic home of fully grown Christian men and women, and a nourishing r¹ our children. So be it. Amen.

ENDNOTES

1. Gary R. Sattler, *God's Glory, Neighbor's Good: A Brief Introduction to the Life and Writings of August Hermann Francke* (Chicago: Covenant Press, 1982), p. 31.

2. David Nyvall and Karl Olsson, *The Evangelical Covenant Church* (Chicago: Covenant Press, 1954), p. 104.

3. Eric G. Hawkinson, *Images in Covenant Beginnings* (Chicago: Covenant Press, 1968), pp. 36f.

CHAPTER 9

What Did God Have in Mind?

The Covenant Companion, February 15, 1983

There is an old saying: "When a man stops, looks up from his work, and asks 'Who am I? And what am I doing here?' things can never be the same again." Minutes, days, years, decades pass. We work and eat and sleep, heads down into our routines like sheep nibbling the grasses of the field, step after thoughtless step carrying us unaware toward places strange to us. If we are lucky, the shepherd's dog will nip us back out of lostness before the lion roars—and leaps! Else it may be quick death for us, or, at least, a frightening night out in the cold. We are not sheep, though we often behave like them. Humans have the power to reflect, to stop what we are doing and look up, to ask the great questions, even though our culture does its best to mislead all but the most trivial: "What shall I buy next?" "Where is the most interesting restaurant?" "Who will win the Super Bowl?"

From long experience, both blessed and bitter, Jews know what must be remembered. At the Passover table, a boy asks the question: "Why is this night different from all other nights in the year?" The answer is the retelling of the story of that exodus of thousands of years ago. The Jewish family remembers Abraham and Isaac and Jacob: where Israel came from, how it was delivered from Egyptian bondage, how Yahweh led it into the wilderness, gave it Torah, and then led it into the Promised Land. A Jew who forgets all that can be no Jew!

And what can we say of us? Have we any real need of more than a nodding acknowledgment of our immediate ancestors in faith? Is any useful purpose served by remembering our origins? "Much," St. Paul would say, "in every way," for we too are the children of an exodus, a mighty migration of forty million of the earth's peoples into another Promised Land. We are here today, and in fellowship today, because our ancestral earth was shaken. Nothing in the world has been the same since that torrential flooding of people into the Western Hemisphere.

Our ancestors had little English, no capital, no safe and assured place of rest, no guarantee of success. Most would never see home again. They had, beside a few personal things in a small sea chest, nothing but hope to satisfy their thirst for land and freedom. Some of them had faith also, having been shocked during the storms at home into asking the primal question: "What must I do to be saved?" Faith they would need, because they were crossing over into strange places, with outlandish names and bewildering customs (many as yet unnamed), seething in the raw chaos of beginnings, dangerous and unpredictable. None of the immigrants knew the end of their story.

In that uncertainty lay great blessings. Among them was the freedom to move about, to experiment. People on the move do not build walls. What would be the point? Instead of walls they had each other, instead of money they had fellowship. And in the fellowship they had Jesus, the one who had saved them, the one who traveled the sea with them, the Lord they had discovered in the midst of the storm and who, in the vast confusions of this new Promised Land, now charged them to witness to their experience of him.

There was another blessing: the instinctive knowledge shared among the immigrants that they were actors in a mighty drama! They had a sense of history played out in daily experience. They were part of something vastly important: without knowing anything of the outcome, they seemed to sense that what they had done and were doing was significant beyond their own immediate destiny. A successful army moves in that spirit—as in fact, does any creative enterprise. If we do not share that conviction today, it is perhaps because we have come to think that what they did was simply obvious.

When the Covenant founders gathered in the Tabernacle in that blizzard-whipped Chicago of February 1885, they saw nothing obvious except the chaos around them. In less than twenty years they had created dozens of churches, two warring synods, a college, several newspapers, and an angry sea of controversy. One of the synods was about to dissolve in constitutional confusion, the college was barely treading water, and a number of churches had seceded from the synods to take an independent position. Engaging demagogues with a thoroughly American eye for opportunity came roaring through the churches producing excitement, theological confusion, and a splintered fellowship. And still the immigrants poured in, flooding the land with problems—and opportunity. No wonder Fred Johnson took as his text for the keynote sermon at this meeting: "I am a companion of all who fear you, of those who keep your precepts" (Psalm 119:63). It was a hope, at the moment nothing more.

But it was a sufficient hope. The companionship of which Johnson spoke came to flower in hundreds of fields from New England to California, from Alaska and China to Africa and Latin America, in places unknown to the founders, in ways wholly unpredictable by anyone in 1885. The companionship lives today, enlarged and enlivened by peoples of diverse ethnic backgrounds and traditions, and shared in congregations, educational institutions, mission fields, and annual meetings.

If we are to recover our ancestral experiences, we must unsheathe our imaginations, enter into the past as participants, and measure its meaning in a realistic but inward way. Are we alive in vast and confusing currents of cultural change? So were they! Do our resources seem limited and poor by the measurement of all that needs to be done? They had almost nothing at all! Do we seem few, pitted against the vast armies of darkness? They were a handful! Are we inadequate? They, too, were ordinary people! Are we confused about the future? So were they! It is by God's mercy that we do not know the future, so that we may live and act in faith. And faith can be fed by memory, above all the memory of the mighty acts of God. For as surely as the Lord God brought Israel out of Egypt, so he swarmed the millions of the world into this new Promised Land. To paraphrase Amos (9:7): "Did I not bring up the Swedes out of the land of Småland, and the Germans from Hesse, and the Irish from Dublin?"

What did God have in mind, bringing all of us here? "God," as Einstein observed, "is often mysterious, never tricky." If we cannot know the ultimate purpose of these vast migrations, continuing as they do today over the whole globe, we may in the very mystery of it sense their importance, and make ourselves alive to the dignity of our own small part in the adventure. Our great danger lies not in uncertainty but in forgetting where we came from and—like children of Israel—simply settling down in Canaan, where experience of the vices of humankind is old and an ancient cynicism spurs faith in all but money and armies as naïve. When we depend upon walls to defend ourselves from attack, when we turn all our energies to accumulating wealth for a secure old age, when we turn life into a continuing search for a better restaurant or a new set of games, we are turning like Israel to Baal and forgetting who saved us. We would then become what so often threatened Israel—pathetic victims of a Philistine whim, a laughing stock in Gath.

But God is faithful, and no more will he forget us than he would forget Israel. Indeed, he will not let us go, wish it as we might in our lazier, more faithless moments. God the gentle Father is also the majestic sovereign of history, working out his purposes in his own way and his own good time. And even though he is mysterious, he leaves his footprints, and they say something of his intentions.

I think he had several things in mind when he stirred our ancestors out of their accustomed places. I think he was determined on a new humankind, available only when old forms could be brought in living form into conjunction with each other. He meant that Swede and German, Irish and Scot, Italian and Russian, Chinese and Japanese, Cambodian and Turk, Korean and Hispanic should meet daily, rub shoulders with each other, and make something new. And I think he was in a relative hurry! See how much and in what powerful ways the earth-environment has changed during the life of our Covenant. My grandfathers drove horses, thought the train something quite new, and one of them, at least, yearned to drive a Model T. My father, born in that world, watched astronauts land on the moon! Our people today are sophisticated in the new technology of travel, communication, healing, and production. They know how to use these brilliant creations. It must therefore be part of our task to enable them to employ these technologies in the service of the kingdom.

I think also that God had children in mind—the future of humankind, and always his messages to the future. No message out of the century past comes more clearly to the present than that the immigrants wanted opportunity, especially for their children. God loves children, wants them fed and cared for, wants them nurtured. The Sunday-school movement of the 1850s was an authentic instinct: all children must have the opportunity for learning, from Scripture to self-awareness, and all the necessary skills between. We have no resource of any kind to compare with the gift of our children. We must give ourselves to their nurture, to their Christian and liberal education, and above all, we must learn to listen to their demands for significant activity, must support them and fund them in their urgent need to find new ways to serve. Inside them is the depth of the future; we must not allow our own pre-occupations to obscure for us their need of support and resources as they work out the meaning of their own existence.

I think also God had the suffering and the oppressed in mind. "For such a king as this," sings the mother of Amahl to the night visitors, "have I waited all my life." Our God is the natural friend of the friendless, the Father of a Son who ate gladly with publicans and sinners, and who suffered, at last, the deathly torment of official power in his own body. All who have been forcibly kept from the table are in the heart of the One born in a stable because there was no room in the inn. Every slave chained to the oar, every orphan sold for labor, every woman sold to men for money, has this God for friend. "Send me your huddled masses, yearning to breathe free," sang Emma Lazarus, in lines long since carved on Liberty, who lifts her lamp above the golden door—New York. How our ancestors waited for their first glimpse of Liberty! The charge to us is clear. We must see to the needs of the suffering, the oppressed. We must find ways of speaking clearly and prophetically to power, even (and perhaps especially) when it is our own. And we must welcome the refugee, the homeless, in the name of our own history.

Finally, I think God had the gospel in mind, that whole good news to all that is humankind. Our Covenant forebears understood themselves to be pilgrims; their context was an imagination and a set of images formed in the whole riches of the Bible. Their first love was Jesus—not the propositional Jesus defined by doctrine, but the living Lord, moving among them with gentle words and healing, with discipline and direction, always in companionship. That their own lives could be so enriched by this living Lord, and that their fellow human beings could still live without any sense of this possibility was to them an intolerable deprivation. For our Covenant fathers and mothers, this was the mission that made them Mission Friends—to tell everyone who would listen about Jesus. It was the central direction in their lives. Who, looking at the developing life of America, could doubt its importance as a mission? And who, looking at the common life of our globe today, can doubt the need of that missional urgency?

Reflecting on his experience of Plymouth Plantation, William

Bradford was later to write: "May not and ought not the children of these fathers rightly say: Our fathers were Englishmen who came over this great ocean, and were ready to perish in this wilderness; but they cried unto the Lord, and he heard their voice, and looked on their adversity, etc. Let them therefore praise the Lord, because he is good and his mercies endure forever."

May we not also give thanks?

CHAPTER 10

The Pietist Schoolman

Essay originally published in Amicus Dei: Essays on Faith
and Friendship, *Philip J. Anderson, ed. (Chicago:
Covenant Publications, 1988), pp. 96-108.*

W hen David Nyvall resigned his position as assistant to Fridolf Risberg in the Swedish division of Chicago Theological Seminary, his purpose was to free himself to work toward a Covenant school. What it cost Nyvall to become the Covenant's schoolman is to be found in Karl Olsson's wryly accurate assessment, reflecting to some degree his own experience, as well as that of the legion of educated Pietists during recent centuries who have struggled to found and maintain schools for the children of their fellowships:

> [Nyvall] left security, status, and almost ideal working conditions (that would have permitted him to carry on his beloved studies) for insecurity, poverty, frequent hostility to educational enterprise, a great deal of personal envy of the educated, and an exhausting schedule of speaking, writing, teaching, and administering. He did this because he believed in the cause of the Covenant and in Covenant education. He never seems to have regretted his step.[1]

Some of this exigency was inseparable from beginnings. No one lives affluently when capital is scarce and tradition thin. What Europe's wandering scholars had suffered during the twelfth- and thirteenth-century infancy of the universities, later schoolmen would have to endure in their turn.[2]

Time and stereotype being what they are, one hesitates to mention Henry Dunster of Harvard and David Nyvall of North Park in the same breath. But no one familiar with the records can doubt that the Massachusetts Bay Puritan schoolman and the Covenant schoolman would have had much to compare with each other, including their forced retirement from office: Dunster (in 1653) because conscience led him to confess publicly his position as a Baptist, Nyvall (in 1905) because conscience compelled him to remain a convinced and honorable Pietist. But overdue tuitions and payment in kind were their daily experience, though 250 years separated their professional lives.[3]

The quickening of Euro-American Protestantism we now call Pietism was on one of its many faces Lutheran.[4] This line runs from Johann Arndt's True Christianity (1605-1609) to Philipp Jakob Spener's Pia Desideria (1675) to Spener's protegé, August Hermann Francke, pastor and professor in Halle/Glaucha (1692-1727). Francke wrote:

> I found among the poor people such coarse and dreadful ignorance that I almost did not know where I should begin to bring to them a firm foundation of their Christianity. . . . So many people went about like cattle without any knowledge of God and divine things, but in particular that so many children, on account of the poverty of their parents, neither attended school nor otherwise enjoyed any good upbringing, but rather grew up in the most shameful ignorance and in all wickedness so that with advancing years they became of no use and therefore gave themselves over to stealing, robbery, and wicked deeds.[5]

Francke began by inviting the poor to devotionals in his parsonage, where he distributed alms. When in 1694 an unexpected sum appeared in the alms box, he used the money to begin a school for poor children, went on to establish an orphanage, a free lunch program for needy university students, a home for widows, a series of new schools for middle- and upper-class children, and the Canstein Press, which in the course of its work printed and distributed more than two million Bibles and other edifying literature. Taken together with the powerful impetus to world missions, these were the Halle Foundations, exemplars to a quickly growing circle of Christian progressives.

Francke the preacher was frequently in hot water with high-church Lutherans; Francke the educator and philanthropic entrepreneur remained in good favor with influential laypersons at the court of Brandenburg who usually responded generously to his pleas for moral and financial support. Pietist schoolmen usually enjoyed more sympathy from kings than from archbishops.[6]

They were also well received by Americans. Stung by orthodox disdain for the New World as "the outer darkness" into which the worthless servant of Matthew 25:30 was to be cast, Cotton Mather (M.A. Harvard, 1681) wrote enthusiastically to Francke in 1717 about the Halle Foundations, declaring that "we Americans here live beyond Ultima Thule, in a country unknown to Strabo and Caesar, but not unknown to Christ," and went on to defend the ecumenical spirit as something deeply shared by "American pietists," among whom he included himself.[7]

Let us remember that Halle was not the only foundation of the 1690s; so also was Yale College,[8] and William and Mary. Obviously, the curve of educational concern was rising, not only among Pietists but among people of other theological views, and in both hemispheres. Whatever labels we use, the Bay Colony Puritans had a concern that Francke shared, and that they had moved to satisfy in the New World sixty years before. As Samuel Eliot Morison says:

> The common school system of early Massachusetts was intended to teach boys to write, cipher, and read the Bible, and that it did. Are we too sophisticated to admit that reading the Bible may be of some use to a people in forming their character, or instructing their taste?[9]

As for Harvard College, its first college laws included the requirement that every student be instructed that "the main end of his life and studies was to know God and Jesus Christ . . . and therefore to lay Christ in the bottom, as the only foundation of all sound knowledge and learning."[10] That the Harvard founders were Puritans and university trained was equally clear; their passion for an educated ministry was at the root of their decision to banish Anne Hutchinson and her party. Had the Hutchinson view prevailed, thinks Morison, there never would have been a Harvard.[11]

Whether German or English, the Pietist schoolman as a type necessarily reflected the character of Pietism as a Christian movement.[12] The Pietist schoolman was usually a university graduate profoundly discontented with the state of the church and determined to see it reformed. He was mainline in theological conviction but hungry and thirsty for living faith experienced in the company of others. He tended to place less emphasis on creed than on Bible, less on erudition than on pastoral care, less on the authority than on the responsibility of the pastoral office. The Pietist schoolman was urgent about his responsibility to the children of common people. Francke loved to say that his duty was twofold: God's glory and neighbor's good. Francke's mentor, Spener, looked forward to "better times in the church," being deeply rooted in a confidence that serious biblical awareness and a new spirit of lay ministration would soften the rigid doctrinal orthodoxies into which the territorial churches had fallen since Luther and Calvin.[13] Nor did Spener hesitate to recommend that Christians debate their theological opponents in the spirit of the Good Samaritan.

Spener's godson, Nikolaus Ludwig Graf von Zinzendorf (1700-1760), equally at home in Germany, Britain, and America, breathed ecumenical generosity and educational innovation:

> Zinzendorf would have nothing to do with the prevailing form of religious education which sought to mold all the children into the same pattern and to demand of them the same inward experiences in a set progressive order. He recognized the manifoldness of life and the individuality of the child. He opposed the tyranny of schemes and methodism. As long as the child is "walking with Jesus" he is being nurtured in the best possible of all schools: "In Herrnhut we do not shape the children," he wrote, "we leave that to the Creator." He was against coercive measures in any branch of the child's education. The modern conception of "teaching as meeting" was implicit in his whole approach.[14]

Zinzendorf's daughter maintained the family tradition in America by opening a school for girls at Ashmead House, Germantown, Pennsylvania, in 1742, attended among others by George Washington's niece, Eleanor Lee.

Eighteenth-century Enlightenment winds blew good news for children and others in need of instruction. To the Pietist concern for an educated ministry and a ministering laity, we may add an increasing secular awareness of the social values of education. Rousseau's *Émile* was first published in 1762. Johann Heinrich Pestalozzi (1746-1827) read it while training for the Lutheran priesthood in Switzerland; together with the memory of his grandfather's careful pastoral attention to the education of his parish children in the canton of Zürich, *Émile* persuaded him of his vocation to children. In 1774 Pestalozzi opened an orphanage to teach neglected children useful life skills, based on pedagogical convictions centered on the natural growth of the child, and illustrated in *Leonard and Gertrude*, a novel first published in 1781.[16] His boarding school at Yverdon, founded in 1805, attracted European attention, not least from the founding father of the *Kindergarten* movement, Friedrich Froebel (1782-1852), whose father was an Old Lutheran pastor in Thuringia.[17]

From Pestalozzi and Froebel, and their enthusiastic advocate, the German reform philosopher Johann Fichte, as well as from his own dismal experiences as a schoolboy, the powerful leader of the Danish national renaissance, Nikolai F. S. Grundtvig (1783-1872) took inspiration and direction. Grundtvig, seriously at odds with the prevailing rationalism of the Danish theological faculties, believed with Froebel that all education must be religious at its base for it to be productive. Against the prevailing pedagogical practice, he desired a method and content for school instruction more natural to the learner. Education, said Grundtvig, must have as its goal "man first, then Christian."[18] Grundtvig was no jovial Enlightenment optimist:

> He had learned from his own experience that human life without Christ is "to worse than the grave cast out":
> "In and of itself, the soul
> Severed from life's spring,
> Like a river cut off from its source,
> Sooner or later runs dry."
> And separated from life's spring man had become. Only in Christ did the spring gush forth anew, in Christ as he was found in the living word in the congregation.[19]

Nor did Grundtvig's vision stop with the education of children. He saw all around him young people and adults who had no hope of a university matriculation, but who for their own sakes and for the future of his beloved Denmark needed access to educational stimulus. His answer: a school for people, eighteen years and older, based upon the same sense of natural and practical order that Pestalozzi and Froebel had advocated for children. Thus were born the "folk high schools,"[20] the first at Rödding in North Schleswig in 1844, the second under Christen Kold at Ryslinge in 1850.[21] The folk high school idea spread quickly to Norway and Finland, less quickly to Sweden. Today these schools number more than 300 throughout Scandinavia.[22]

The first national provision for common schooling in Sweden dates from 1842, the year in which George Scott was driven from Sweden, handing over his infant religious monthly, *Pietisten*, to his young assistant, Carl Olof Rosenius (1816-1868). The very word "Pietist" was so obnoxious to high-church Swedes that Archbishop Wingård pleaded with Scott to choose another title.[23] The journal, as Rosenius shaped it, was itself a schooling in biblical piety for the growing conventicle movement in the Swedish countryside, for which Rosenius became, by degrees, mentor and prophet.[24] More perhaps than any other, Rosenius led his people back to Luther, and through Luther to serious biblical study of narrative and argument. It is not an exaggeration to call him the biblical schoolmaster to the *läsare* movement; he did not begin it, he instructed it. Around Rosenius gathered Swedish priests and laity with a passion for church reform, the circle that would produce in 1856 the National Evangelical Foundation, almost—if not quite—a bow back to Spener.

Among the humbler of this circle was P. A. Ahlberg (1823-1887), between 1861 and 1875 the master of Ahlsborg—a school in Vetlanda, Småland, for boys, colporteurs, and candidates for the North American ministry. Ahlberg remembered his own school days: "To read and to weep—floggings and long lessons—clarified mostly with the cane."[25] Clearly Ahlberg's Vimmerby schoolmaster had not heard of Zinzendorf, Pestalozzi, or Grundtvig; nor, possibly, would he have listened had he heard. But we have Erik August Skogsbergh's recollections of happy days with Pastor Ahlberg (even though he thought Ahlberg too much bound to the law), getting homiletic instruction some years before his emigration in 1876 to Chicago.[26]

That Pietism as a folk movement could create its own schools was demonstrated by the widow Maria Nilsdotter of Vall, Värmland, when she began a Sunday school on her farm in 1850, and some years later expanded it into an orphanage-school with the support of her son Carl Johan and others in the Karlskoga parish. No Francke in either education or connection, her instincts ran in the same directions and her energies dominated the landscape around her.[27] Schools remained a central concern to Carl Johan Nyvall as he progressed through his tutelage as colporteur for the National Evangelical Foundation, to itinerant preacher, to founding spirit of the Värmland Ansgar Society, to one of the handful of founders of the Swedish Mission Covenant in 1878. David Nyvall believed that his father's foremost concern in the establishment of the Covenant was to assure organizational support for schools.[28]

David Nyvall at sixteen sent off a letter to his father's great friend Paul Peter Waldenström, asking advice on the best way to become a poet. Waldenström replied immediately:

> If you follow my advice, you will not fantasize away your time with novels and such stuff, but will settle yourself down to those studies demanded by a proper and basic *Studentexamen*. If God intends you to be a poet, you cannot become one without study, and if someday you become one, you will find in God's will rich fields for the greatest poetic gifts if you wish wholly to serve the Lord.[29]

Thus began a seminal relationship between a visionary boy and the linguist-theologian-free church preacher that would continue through bright and stormy weather on two continents. Nyvall, reflecting, declared that his studies under Waldenström at Gävle revealed a teacher of unequalled clarity: "His way of paraphrasing and condensing Norbeck's *Dogmatics* was astonishing in its effect. The most unimaginable became self-evident as he worked with it. And as a rule it took him one line to clarify what the book took ten lines to obscure."[30]

But clarity for the living future might be another matter. We do not know why David Nyvall entered medical studies at Uppsala; we do know that he appeared in Chicago during the summer of 1886, distressed and forlorn. He and his father explained only that he was visiting. But the visit turned into an emigration, the visitor into a greenhorn in search of his own Promised Land. He was, however, not alone. The river of Swedes flowing into America was at high flood. Moreover, a generation of predecessors had worked their way through the confusions of American life and had formed the North American Covenant in 1885, not without the influence of Nyvall's father.

Some confusion remained. Like other religiously serious Swedes, Covenanters had to face the educational question presented by the absence in America of a state church and its associated institutions.

Ethnicity, theology, and fellowship went into the search for an appropriate form.[31] The Covenant at its organizational meeting in 1885 had accepted a generous offer from American Congregationalists to provide theological training for ministerial candidates in a Scandinavian department at Chicago Theological Seminary. Was this "Risberg's School" an adequate solution? Fridolf Risberg, personally selected in consultation with Waldenström by C. A. Björk, thought so and remained faithful to his original understanding with the seminary until the department was disbanded in 1917. Others were not so sure. Some complained that the selection and admission of ministerial candidates were not under Covenant control. Others, including Nyvall, looked in vain for educational opportunities for Covenant young people without ministerial vocation.

That is why Nyvall, after two happy years as Risberg's assistant during 1888-1890, returned to Skogsbergh's school in Minneapolis, a school for immigrants begun in 1884:

> It was a humble enterprise, to be sure. We gathered in an empty store in a then outlying part of the town where Lindblade taught English and Business and I taught, in Swedish, everything that I could persuade anybody to learn. . . . It was, in all its poverty and its almost total lack of organization, an independent school, standing under obligation to no other denomination and absolutely free to accept students and adopt methods that seemed best fitted to the ends in view. The work was not in vain.[32]

It might have been Halle/Glaucha two centuries earlier, another attempt at "God's glory, neighbor's good." Nor did it stop for the Covenant with Nyvall.

Karl Olsson, coming to the North Park presidency in 1959, chose to grapple with traditional Pietist themes in his inaugural address titled "Divine Foolishness and Human Learning."[33] "Is it possible," he asks, "that Paul has anything to say to schoolmen?" At the center he places the traditional *Wiedergeburt* of Pietism, quoting Blaise Pascal's journal of midnight visitation: "FIRE—God of Abraham, God of Isaac, God of Jacob, not of the philosophers and scholars. Certitude." Against this incommensurable experience, Olsson places Paul's complaint that Jews are seeking for a sign, Greeks for wisdom. "If the pursuit of a sign or the pursuit of learning is thought to control human history, then God has become a captive God devoid of sovereignty and freedom." Where then is the solution? Some schools, embarrassed by traditional theology, have become secular. Others have become moralistic and doctrinaire. "This school," says Olsson, "adheres to its Christian heritage not merely because it desires the redemption of man but because it desires the redemption of learning through the foolishness of God."

> God will continue, no matter how much we may protest, to choose the foolish to shame the wise, the weak to shame the strong, and the low, the despised, and the nothing of this world to bring to nothing the things that are. So inscrutable is his wisdom and his ways past finding out. *To him alone be the glory now and forever.*

It is in the nature of the inspiration that took Pietism as its form that its work is never finished, not at least until God's kingdom is completed. That work required, and requires, the schoolman, the one whom Nyvall called the skylark—on whose wings one first discerns the dawning of the new day.

ENDNOTES

1. David Nyvall and Karl A. Olsson, *The Evangelical Covenant Church* (Chicago: Covenant Press, 1954), p. 64, n. 21.

2. The term "schoolman" is traditionally derived from these medieval teachers of philosophy and theology. It is used in this paper to describe the later adaptions of this educational tradition and is not intended to be exclusive in language or tone; rather, it recognizes the metaphor and self-understanding of the specific historical contexts.

3. Dunster (1609-1660) M. A. Magdalene College, Cambridge, emigrated to Massachusetts Bay in 1640 and was immediately appointed president of Harvard. Samuel Eliot Morison, *Builders of the Bay Colony* (Boston: Houghton Mifflin, 1930), pp. 183-216, presents a lively and loving portrait. The reluctance of the Massachusetts General Court to remove him from office is clearly documented. Nevertheless, antipedobaptism was considered unacceptable radicalism, especially in the leader of Harvard.

4. One should not neglect, however, Chasidism as well as French Jansenism. See Martin Buber, *The Origin and Meaning of Hasidism*, Maurice Friedman, ed. and trans. (New York: Horizon Press, 1960); and F. Ernest Stoeffler, *The Rise of Evangelical Pietism* (Leiden: E. J. Brill, 1965).

5. Quoted in Gary R. Sattler, *God's Glory, Neighbor's Good* (Chicago: Covenant Press, 1982), p. 48. This work offers a concise description of Francke's world-famous "Foundations" (pp. 47-67).

6. The University of Halle was itself a foundation by Frederick III of Branden-burg. Compare the experience of N. F. S. Grundtvig with Christian III of Denmark, and of P. P. Waldenström with Oscar II of Sweden.

7. Ernst Benz, "Ecumenical Relations between Boston Puritanism and German Pietism: Cotton Mather and August Jermann Francke," *Harvard Theological Review*, 54 (1961), 165, 171. One may suspect diplomacy in Mather's language without entirely discounting his willingness to be identified with Francke's efforts. The point of contact between the two was the court chaplain to George of Denmark, Prince Consort of Queen Anne, Pastor Anton Wilhelm Boehm, who played a role in London uncannily parallel to that played in Stockholm in the 1830s by the Wesleyan pastor George Scott. For a full treatment of Mather and Pietism, see Richard L. Lovelace, *The American Pietism of Cotton Mather: Origins of American Evangelicalism* (Grand Rapids: Eerdmans, 1979).

8. With an original grant from Elihu Yale obtained through the good offices of Cotton Mather! See Roland Bainton, *Yale and the Ministry* (New York: Harper and Row, 1957), pp. 6-9.

9. Morison, *Builders of the Bay Colony*, p. 187.

10. Quoted in Samuel E. Morison, *The Founding of Harvard College* (Cambridge: Harvard University Press, 1935), p. 251.

11. Ibid., pp. 171-180, for Morison's discussion of the real options.

12. Debate during the past generation about the boundaries of Peitism has stabilized our categories. An excellent summary of the present understanding is in F. Ernest Stoeffler, "Pietism: Its Message, Early Manifestations, and Significance," *The Covenant Quarterly*, 34 (1976), 3-24. The reader will do well to bear in mind Stoeffler's opening sentence: "Historical movements have fuzzy edges."

13. Spener's vision of the Pietist program is concisely summarized in K. James Stein, *Philipp Jakob Spener: Pietist Patriarch* (Chicago: Covenant Press, 1986), pp. 93-103. See also Manfred W. Kohl, "Spener's Pia Desideria—The *Programmschrift* of Pietiem," *The Covenant Quarterly*, 34 (1976), 61-78.

14. A. J. Lewis, *Zinzendorf the Ecumenical Pioneer* (Philadelphia: Westminster Press, 1962), pp. 172f.

15. Ibid., p.174. Lewis quotes E. E. and L. R. Gray, *Wilderness Christians*, p. 331: "Many twentieth-century educational programmes were inaugurated in eighteenth-century Moravian schools. Parent-teachers' meeting, community-school association, educational and vocational guidance, and student participation in school management were common practice as early as 1750."

16. A. Pinloche, *Pestalozzi and the Foundation of the Modern Elelmentary School* (New York: Scribner 1901) is a reasonable summary. See also Eva Channing, trans. and ed., *Pestalozzi's Leonard and Gertrude* (New York: D. C. Heath, 1885). The pastor "no longer allowed the children to learn any long prayers by rote, saying this was contrary to the spirit of Christianity, and the express injunctions of their Savior" (p. 156f).

17. Robert B. Downs, *Friedrich Froebel* (Boston: Twayne, 1978).

18. Hal Koch, *Grundtvig*, Llewellyn Jones, trans. (Yellow Springs, Ohio: Antioch Press, 1952), pp. 151-165. Jones freely translates one of Grundtvig's poems: "If we do not feel in our hearts,/ We are sprung of heaven's race,/ If we

cannot feel with sorrow,/ That we have become debased,/ Then we only make mock of the word/That God will redeem us and give/Rebirth as his own children."
19. Ibid., p. 152.
20. Not to be understood in the sense of American secondary schools. There were to be adult education foundations, small residential schools built around the idea of mutual communication and practical educational purpose. "High" meant, therefore, only "advanced," while "folk" might find the experience useful. Grundtvig himself founded no schools, though he projected many.
21. Roar Skovmand, "Grundtvig and the Folk High School Movement," in Christen Thodberg and Anders P. Thyssen, eds., N. F. S. Grundtvig: Traditiona & Renewal, Edward Broadbridge, trans. (Copenhagen: Det Danske Selskab, 1983), pp. 321-343.
22. Was it Grundtvig's passionate insistence on the importance of the Danish mother tongue that inspired the pedagogically revolutionary discoveries of Jens O. H. Jesperson (1860-1943), a linguist who insisted that foreign languages must be taught as children learn their own, by using it, even before they know what they are saying? One of the scandals of American education in the twentieth century is that few Amreicans (outside the Peace Corps) have paid much attention to Jesperson's methods.
23. Gunnar Westin, George Scott och hans verksamhet i Sverige (Stockholm: Svenska kyrkans diakonistyrelses bokförlag, 1929), p. 622.
24. Karl A. Olsson, By One Spirit (Chicago: Covenant Press, 1962), pp. 52-58, provides a graphic description of the conventicle practice during these years. By 1855 Pietisten had a monthly circulation of 7,000, compared to Aftonbladet (the most popular liberal paper in the country) at 4,000 (Erland Sundstom, Trossamfund i det svenska samhället [Stockholm: tidnes förlag, 1952], pp.70-71). And that figure needs a mulitplier; the paper was often shared, one subscriber per conventicle!
25. E. J. Ekman, Den inre missionens historia (Stockhom: E. J. Ekmans förlsgs-expedition, 1896-1902), II:2, p. 1141.
26. E. August Skogsbergh, Minnen och upplevelser (Minneapolis: Veckobladets tryckeri [1923]), pp. 51-58.
27. David Nyvall, My Father's Testament, Eric G. Hawkinson, trans. (Chicago: Covenant Press, 1974), pp. 28ff., 63-73.
28. Ibid., pp. 153-58.
29. The letter in Waldenström's hand is reproduced in David Nyvall, "Waldenström som lärare," in A. Ohlden, ed., Lector P. Waldenström (Uppsala: J. A. Lindblads förlag, 1917), p. 65. It is dated 18 September 1879.
30. Ibid., p.67.
31. Swedish Americans had already expended tremendous energies in establishing appropriate schools. A listing of surviving schools might be a helpful reminder:
Augustana, Rock Island, Illinois (1869)
Augustana, Sioux Falls, South Dakota (1861)
Gustavus Adolphus, St. Peter, Minnesota (1862)
Bethel, St. Paul, Minnesota (1871)

Bethany, Lindsborg, Kansas (1881)
Pacific Lutheran, Tacoma, Washington (1890)
North Park, Chicago, Illinois (1891)
Upsala, East Orange, New Jersey (1893)
Trinity, Deerfield, Illinois (1897)

An incomplete listing of colleges not surviving includes:
Ansgar, Knoxville, Illinois (1975-1884)
Martin Luther, Chicago, Illinois (1893-1895)
Texas Wesleyan, Austin, Texas (1911-1931)
Trinity, Round Rock, Texas (closed 1929)
Walden, McPherson, Kansis (1907-1912)

To these add a substantial number of secondary institutions. See, for instance, Emeroy Johnson, "Swedish Academies in Minnesota," *Swedish Pioneer Historical Quarterly*, 32 (1981), 20-40.

32. Quoted in Leland H. Carlson, *A History of North Park College* (Chicago: North Park College, 1941), pp. 24f. Nyvall had spent 1887-1888 with Skogsbergh in Minneapolis.

33. The text is printed in *Pietisten*, 3, No. 1 (1988); it was also published separately following the inauguaration in 1959 by North Park College.

III

FIRST QUESTIONS

Editors' note: Zenos Hawkinson understood Pietism essentially to be a movement that sought wholeness in life. He believed deeply that this required a discussion and theological understanding of our working life, since so much of our life is taken by our daily labor. We present two articles, written twenty years apart, that raise these "first questions." Does the church have a place in the discussion about work? What truly is "Christian" work? How might the church have a prophetic voice within an economy that is voracious in its appetite, nourished by marketing hype, and that places primary demands on our time and energies? How do we integrate the working life into the life of faith and worship? What are the marks of wholeness that might provide a point of reference for this discussion?

CHAPTER 11

I Will Serve the Work

The Covenant Companion, November 3, 1967

W hen I was a boy, people were always talking about going into "full-time Christian service." Evidently it was important, because the people who did it got consecrated in solemn ceremonies. There was a lot of laying on of hands and receptions, both coming and going, and usually a collection. The rest of us were pledged to stay home and support the "full-timers." But we were never consecrated—maybe because there were so many of us.

Anyhow, I never saw a carpenter consecrated unless he agreed to go to a mission field. I do not suppose any of our carpenters expected to be consecrated if they just stayed in Chicago or Moline and built houses and cabinets. Sometimes if the carpenter became a Sunday-school superintendent, he would be asked to stand up on Sunday morning and be dedicated, but not because he was a carpenter. And the same for others who were bricklayers and druggists, insurance men and doctors.

So I learned that there was a difference between Christian work and other kinds of work. Usually the other kinds paid more. The "full-timers" had shiny pants and were not supposed to worry about money. But at least they were consecrated, and I did not doubt they would have the inside track on Judgment Day. The others had to get their blessing by giving generously. I had heard a great deal about tithing. I even heard a man who said he had discovered that if he gave 90 percent to the Lord, the 10 percent remaining would get constantly bigger. I thought that if that were true, it would be a sure fire way to riches. But when I tried it, I went immediately bankrupt.

The point is that there was clearly a gulf between two worlds of work. Beyond telling me the usual thing about honesty and thrift and sobriety, the church told me very little about how I should conduct myself toward my job, where I could expect to spend the majority of my time and energy. I say the church told me little, as a church. The people of that community told me a great deal. Sunday-school teachers told me I would have to work because of Adam's sin. I did not brood about that doom because I lived among people who loved to work, most of them in small businesses and crafts, with roots firmly planted in the old soil. It was still a face-to-face community where people knew each other's skills and characters with something like fullness, and that was enough to keep us healthy. Our common life was stronger and more sufficient than our thought.

The revolution we are living through these days has taken away that healthy community and left us helpless to understand the contradictions dividing us. Taught from boyhood to work hard, save, pay cash, and abstain, I am now urged to retire early, spend, use my credit line, and consume. The boy heard people say proudly, "That'll last a lifetime." Today we hear that this is dangerous to the economy, which wants a lot of early obsolescence.

The modern firm wants my undivided loyalty and moves me about the country like a shuttlecock so I can never send down competing roots. If I produce first-quality goods, I face early bankruptcy, and unless I employ manipulative advertising, my goods will get dusty on the shelves. If I produce too quickly, the union agent will slow me down, and if I demand decent materials for my craftsmanship, I will be fired.

Told that only work is meaningful and now told that I must retire, what am I to do with myself? I have the feeling that these and dozens of similar questions ought to have a Christian response. I know there are dangers here. Some serious Christians declare the sweaty world of work off-limits for Christian thought. Others just brush off some brand of utopianism, paste a Christian label on it, and declare firmly that people "ought to be nice." Either way, I cannot be one man at worship and a different one at work, and it seems to me that ought to be the test. A really Christian response would bring me toward wholeness.

We should have been consecrating the carpenter. We should have been telling him, as Dorothy Sayers remarked, that bad carpentry is an insult to God. For "no crooked table legs or ill-fitting drawers ever, I dare swear, came out of the carpenter's shop at Nazareth." If St. Paul's tents leaked, how can I take the epistles seriously? Mechanics singing psalms and botching the job, teachers opening with prayers and trotting out the tired old lectures, businessmen displaying "Christian" labels but cutting the specifications where it will not be seen—we are in the same danger of judgment as those who approach the Holy Table carelessly. For the bench is where the Word becomes flesh. It is revealed by the way one works at the bench, whether a person really believes "in him whom the Father hath sent." Words are cheap if they take no body. Men and women who have been at the cross will have to offer more than words as their proper worship.

So I think this is one authentic Christian response: "I will not make junk." Junk is bad for those who make it, bad for those who use it. It is made of things God made but bent and twisted away from their intended purpose by our darkness. It is the same with people. God made them to serve his purposes, to do his work. But they listen to other voices. A man gifted to drive a cab becomes a banker instead. Today he is an "important" man, and desperately unhappy, for he has violated the grain of his being. A great lady in our church once gave public thanks for her garbage man, and it struck me that it may be harder to find good garbage men than millionaires. My nephew, who knows a first-class garbage man and loves him, is closer to the kingdom than the rest of us.

Here is another authentic Christian response: "I will not be a snob." Perfect work is not a question of size or kind but of character. Perfection equals perfection, as infinity equals infinity. It is God who created us and gifted us to work in differing scales and with differing materials. He made the horse and the ass, but Jesus chose the ass for his ride into Jerusalem—and the animal did his job. There will be trumpets for him, whether we like it or not. But the ass did not know about the trumpets, and he will be surprised. If you are working for trumpets, you will be surprised too, unpleasantly, I am afraid. Maybe you already have been. People working for gratitude usually spend more time listening than working. If your head is always turned to see how people are taking you, how can you work well? The authentic Christian response here is: "I will serve the work." The true reward of honest work is in seeing its perfection. God himself looked and saw that it was good. Granting our inescapable imperfections, we ought to have something of the same feeling.

Here is a test: Is what you are doing so absorbing; is the occasional job of fulfillment so rewarding that you are sometimes surprised that other people are willing to pay you for doing what you are doing? If not, if you feel perpetually unrewarded, unappreciated, misunderstood, you are probably not serving the work, or you are trying to serve the work for which you were not gifted.

Either way, your danger is great. For none of us is an accident. And while God may have intended a useful suffering for us, he never intended meaninglessness. Not if he is as Jesus said he is, and not if Jesus Christ is Lord. But there is a Dark Lord, and his method is meaninglessness. And we have surrendered more territory to him than we needed to. That ground must be won back, where we work, because everyone who serves Jesus Christ is in full-time service—if serving where one is put.

CHAPTER 12

He Satisfies Our Strength with Labor

The Covenant Companion, September 1988

On the wall above my desk hangs a hand-illumination done years ago to a text written by my father, Eric. I read it often these days, with a growing appreciation:

> God acts in many contexts. He satisfies
> our physical hunger with bread,
> our thirst with water,
> our intellectual curiosity with knowledge,
> our loneliness with loved ones and friends,
> our sickness with medicine,
> our weariness with sleep, and
> our strength with labor.

That final line invites understanding, especially from one like me, recently retired: *he satisfies our strength with labor.*

Not difficult, is it, to pity the hungry, thirsty, lonely, sick, weary? But why pity those, "retired" or not, whose strength is unsatisfied by a suitable labor? Why not instead congratulate them, those fortunate human beings who have strengths left over, saved in the bank as it were, for a rainy day? Is not that what retirement really means: getting the nose off the stone, getting the feet off the treadmill and on to the ottoman?

The answer we give depends a lot on how we have worked. A person who has spent half a lifetime in bondage to a meaningless drudgery just to get a paycheck may well be forgiven his or her disposition to think of labor in any form as simply the accursed result of original sin. Do not try to tell these people that God has given them labor as a mercy.

Not unless you want them to misunderstand God—or unless you mean to frighten them into working for you at substandard wages. Our economic culture has done its share of both at considerable human cost.

But what of people like me, doing things we were born to do (and thus loved to do), enjoying jobs filled with challenge and variety, working toward valuable goals together with delightful (if not always perfect) people—and actually being paid for our efforts? For us fortunate ones, work was never really a question of money. We had to have money to live, of course, but had we been able to afford it, many of us would have paid others for the privilege of doing what we enjoyed; at the very least, we might well have worked for no money at all. The late Dorothy Sayers spoke for us when she wrote: "Work is not something we do to live; it is something we live to do." That word has in it the ring of good news. We are somewhere in the true depths of ourselves as human beings when we realize that we need meaningful labor just as we need sleep, bread, and water.

Why do we need meaningful labor? Why, because it is in our labor that we chiefly glorify God; it is the offering of our available strength to the One who created us. If a human being has spent his or her entire week goofing off, has made nothing lovely to contemplate, how shall he or she come into the courts of the Lord on the Sabbath with a tongue fit to praise the Creator of the universe?

Let us be careful. God does not love us because we have been faithful at our labor, much less because we praise him with empty words. The best work of a transcendent genius is a poor thing compared to the handiwork of God. We do not work to earn God's approval. We work because a loving Father has gotten through to us with his love, and in the joy of that recognition, we do what we can in our limited ways, confident that as once we brought our childish scrawls to wise and loving parents we may bring the flawed offerings of our mature strength to him as a sign of our love and praise. That is what Chesterton meant when he said, "Anything worth doing is worth doing badly." We cannot be perfect. Therefore we can work. Joyfully.

In the world as God intended it, every human being would have good work to do—good work meaning something with usefulness attached to it, and deep pleasure in the doing of it, a labor appropriate to every strength. In that world, the measure of a man or a woman would be the quality of their work. A joyfully effective street-sweeper would be honored before a slovenly manager, an honest carpenter before a crooked king.

Indeed, slovenly managers and crooked kings could not exist in the world as God intended it. In our bent world they are legion. An arrogant elite supported by armies of lawyers and accountants arranges the industrial and commercial work of the world not to provide satisfying labor to human beings—or even to produce a quality product—but to maximize next quarter's bottom line to satisfy a childishly impatient stock market. That done, they vote themselves congratulatory bonuses of obscene magnitude—and close another plant—complaining all the while about the welfare budget while their toadies in the Congress design them yet another tax-break.

Meantime, how silent is Mother Church! Fearful of offending powerful people, she raises no standard to which honest labor can rally, preaches no Isaianic vision of a world in which lion and lamb lie peacefully together. Worldwide she rushes about adopting leadership models and operating procedures copied verbatim from the bent world in which she lives. She leaves it to secular prophets—Tom Peters, Gyllenhammar of Volvo, Janszon of SAS, a thousand Japanese corporate leaders whose names I do not know—to demonstrate the self-defeating absurdities in which we seem to be trapped.

Forty-five years ago, Sayers assigned a division of responsibility that seems, if anything, even more valid on this Labor Day: "It is the task of the Church to see to it that the work serves the world; it is the task of the worker to serve the work." This because the great reward to a good worker is to behold the work, as God looked at his creation and pronounced it good. Should you doubt that wisdom, you have never seen a craftsman's face when he or she has completed a good piece.

With all my heart I believe that a human being deprived of satisfying labor (no matter how much money he or she makes) is being sickened as surely as if he or she lived on a radioactive dump. What labor is satisfying to an individual is beyond our power of generalization or prediction, but the answer to that question lies inside the person; good sense suggests that each worker come forward with his or her own answer, and that society take his answer as a mandate to provide the work which satisfies his or her strength. A really good manager has learned to listen to people, and arranges affairs according to their strengths. A bad manager puts square pegs in round holes according to his or her own preconceived notions.

We who have "retired" from meaningful jobs know this instinctively. Liberated from the pressures and manipulations of the conventional workplace, we find ourselves unusually free to choose how we shall work and where. Bad managers are threatened by our freedom and shy away from us, knowing that by their usual categories we are "unmanageable." Good managers see in us strengths and talents in short supply, and are eager to use us in mutually agreeable ways.

Therefore we have a special responsibility to our world: to make a continuing demonstration of the value of good work; to stand unmistakably for quality against the surrounding ocean of junk; and to insist on the freedom and dignity of the worker in his or her work, as a sign from God. As a teacher, I saw my students in all their particularity as messages from God, long before the words of Count Zinzendorf confirmed my Covenant instincts: "In Herrnhut we do not shape the children. We leave that to the Creator." As a retired craftsman, it is my responsibility to speak and act for the dignity of coming generations who, like me, children of a loving Father, need nothing so much as worthy labor to satisfy their strength.

Editors' note: It is not difficult for the church to take jabs at prevailing culture, to point out the values that distinguish the kingdom of God from the kingdom of the world. There is a tension here. As a Pietist, Zenos Hawkinson believed that such tension was intrinsic, if not, in fact, necessary. Such tension could be creative if faced honestly. However, he argued, before we rush to judge the world, we should first look honestly and thoroughly at ourselves. This is a "first question!" "Shall all things come under the judgment of God, or shall they not?" In this piece, written almost forty years ago, he raises the concerns of biblical and theological illiteracy within the church. This growing problem leads him to focus upon the relationship between the pastor and the congregation. What should the laity ask of the clergy, and what are the obligations of the laity to the pastor? Where does our mutual accountability lie? These are ancient questions as well as central concerns with historic Pietism. They continue to press themselves upon us today. This article was written in response to Irving Lambert's "Tension between Faith, Culture Is a Condition of the New Life," published a week earlier in the Companion. *It should be noted that this was written thirteen years before the Covenant Church approved the ordination of women.*

CHAPTER 13

Little Serious Tension Exists between the Christian and the World

The Covenant Companion, May 17, 1963

M r. Irving Lambert's argument in last week's *Companion* was that there must be a tension between the Christian and the world. My argument is that there is little serious tension between the Christian and the world. By serious tension, I mean differences resulting from a head-on challenge to the world's claim to govern itself by its own lights. Our practice gives evidence that both pastors and laity are confused today about the center of the battle. The basic question is: shall all things come under the judgment of God, or shall they not? The question facing us is whether we wholeheartedly acknowledge the sovereignty, the authority of God, over the universe, the world, and all things in it, including ourselves.

Consider our prevailing biblical illiteracy. Our communal life as a Covenant Church is based upon the cardinal tenet that God's revelation of himself is ultimately and perfectly expressed in Jesus Christ, our Lord, and in that witness to him we know as the Bible. We own the book and we cull from it texts here and there with which to confound our opponents, but the layperson among us who pays to the Bible the compliment of serious and systematic study is a rare bird. If, as we complain, there is not enough time for this in modern life, that is commentary enough on our true situation.

And we are perpetuating the scandal among our children. They spend twenty-five hours a week in expensive and highly professional school surroundings, by which the world insures that its canons of cultural authority will be successfully transmitted to another generation. They spend another five to ten hours a week absorbing the cultural standards of our time from TV.

But their exposure to biblical instruction is a pitiful one—half or three-quarters of an hour on Sunday morning, taught by an imperfectly prepared teacher from random materials in a room distinguished by is unsuitability for pedagogical purposes. That the child gets even this much is a tribute to the devotion of a very few lonely souls who stand like Dutch boys with a finger in the dike.

In our Covenant Church today biblical education is an intellectual slum, a bitter satire on our public confession that the Bible is the word of God. Nor is our record for theological sophistication more admirable. It is not theology that saves humankind from its sins, but the one who is saved must think about God, and theology is thinking about God. Go to any church and ask the lay leaders to explain the Trinity, to explain the atonement, and then prepare for an embarrassed silence. These persons can quote you the market futures at the drop of a hat, explain from memory the most abstruse problems in mechanics or electricity, or provide you on request an excellent survey of management-labor problems, but in matters theological—uninstructed and opinionated as any small child.

Call him Democrat; he will flare up. Call her Socinian, an infinitely more serious matter to the Christian; she will only shrug. We do not complain that there is no uniformity in our doctrine. We complain that we do not even share that level of awareness that makes doctrinal conversation profitable to the spirit. If we are indifferent to the Bible and to Christian doctrine, how can we be surprised by our regular indifference to the regular health and discipline of the church's life? Who among us, stiff-necked as we are, will submit themselves or their churches to the demands of vocation? Who is to tell *me*, sovereign layman that I am, what I am to give of my talents and my money to the life of the community? And who has the nerve to demand from my congregation an even rudimentary budgetary loyalty to the life of the larger church— the conference and the denomination?

None of us thinks it strange that people in secular society may be imprisoned for failing to pay their taxes, or refusing to obey traffic laws, even for refusing military service. To all these iron disciplines we submit. But to the discipline of God, as expressed in and through the regularly constituted channels of his church, to this we will not submit. For my opinion, as a sovereign layperson, is as good as any other, whether or not I take any trouble to instruct myself. But the truth is this: I am not sovereign. God is sovereign. I am bound to admit sooner or later that it is he who disposes, not I or any number of my friends.

As a layperson, I must be told this with an authority that cannot be denied, and the one who bears primary responsibility for telling me is my pastor. This is an awful vocation: to bring me, as preacher, a Word from God; to bring me, as pastor, the guidance and the comfort I need as one who is needy; to bring me, as priest, the awful mystery of the sacraments; and to put me, as prophet, under a terrible judgment. When I need correction, and my pastor does not correct me, he has failed me before God. When I need instruction, and he does not instruct me, he has left me ignorant before the Most High. When I need consolation, and he leaves me uncomforted, he has left me without the only comfort with which I can truly be comforted.

But see how we speak of a man who bears this unbearable calling: we speak of "hiring" a pastor! To accept this nearly blasphemous conception of his calling is not meekness in a pastor: it is servility. Pastors must rise up in holy indignation against this cheapening of the holy office, for it is not the humiliation of the person but of the office, which is involved. When he speaks of God's judgment, the pastor must demand and receive obedience to it as he is himself obedient to it, and a congregation that refuses a just obedience should be refused the offices of a pastor until it accepts a just discipline. For their part, lay people must demand that their pastors speak for God, with his authority, when led by the Holy Spirit to do so.

Pastors believe that a certain plainness of speech under conviction may endanger their ministerial careers. There is truth in this, and this is no compliment to either laity or pastorate. A lazy, opinionated, tyrannical, or whimsical pastor must also be brought under the discipline of the church, and that properly and promptly. God's call is not to be trifled with, or questioned, but unfaithfulness to it must not be allowed to continue on sentimental grounds. For the sovereignty of God, like the terrible blazing of the sun, is a matter of life and death to us all. What we call for, as lay people, is a renewed sense of the shortness of time in which we may repent, and the immediate need of a personal and corporate repentance, that grace may once more abound among us.

For the freedom we have prized in the Covenant Church is granted by our Father only to those who are faithful to hear his word and do his will. And much of what we have called freedom—indifference, vacillation, even treachery—is not freedom at all, but the darkness with which God hardened the heart of Pharaoh, a prelude to disaster, an invitation to the iron broom of Assyria that shall sweep us without mercy.

Editors' note: The hymnody of the Covenant Church is filled with images of the pilgrim. These songs gave voice to the personal experiences of uprooting and of building a life in a new land. The life of the pilgrim, however, became a deeper metaphor for the Christian life, a joyful life to be sure, yet tinged with yearning for a homeland where the vast upheavals are finally quieted into a lasting and eternal belonging. Zenos Hawkinson loved to sing these hymns and gave himself to a number of their translations. The following song reflecting the pilgrim's life, was written by Nils Frykman, and appeared in the 1909 Covenant hymnal, Sions Basun (#676). It was jointly translated by Zenos and his father, Eric.

CHAPTER 14

This Earth Is Not My Homeland

This earth is not my homeland; 'mid sorrows and despair
I am, just like my fathers, a guest and stranger here.
But in my Father's kingdom a dwelling waits for me—
Unequaled by all earthly pavilions.

Chorus:
Blessed home! City bright!
Where angels joyfully sing,
O what peace! O what joy!
Within the crystal portals of heaven.

As sailors in the tempest look longingly toward land,
So long I for my homeland on heaven's quiet strand:
Where stormy roaring ceases and breakers cannot reach,
Where no one's heart is broken and hopeless.

T'will be a goodly winning to leave this earthly fold,
And with the saints be walking on streets of purest gold.
With joy we join the chorus in heaven's newest song,
Pure melody perfected among us.

EPILOGUE

CHAPTER 15

A Statement about Myself to My Fellow Pilgrims

A Letter to the North Park College Faculty, March 26, 1976

One of the most important sentences I ever read came in an essay by Dorothy Sayers ("Why Work?" *Creed or Chaos*) on the Christian and his work: "No crooked table-legs or ill-fitting drawers ever, I dare swear, came out of the carpenter's shop at Nazareth. Nor, if they did, could anyone believe that they were made by the same hand that made heaven and earth." It came to me not as something new but as something bred in me long ago, at least as long ago as my grandfather's smithy and my father's pulpit. We work to live, and in the quality of our work is the quality of our life. To do less than to pour ourselves totally into our work, to intend less than (if not to achieve) perfect work, is to commit blasphemy. *Incarnatus est:* I seek to glorify God in my work, and in my work the word becomes flesh.

God forgive me! He knows (better than my colleagues) how often the intention has failed, not to mention the achievement. I *have* responded to his glorious creation by coming in at 10:10 a.m. with a piece of junk, disguised, of course (I am a professional, after all) by a thin plating of shiny chrome or sanded gobs of plastic wood, a piece of work produced to cost rather than quality. Neither theological ortho-doxy nor a sentimental appeal to humanity can save me from that damnation. Nothing but the costly grace of the carpenter's shop and the cross can forgive uncaring sloppiness. I have needed this forgiveness many times.

That is what burns in me, and has burned in me since my awakening: the drive for incarnation. I do not want to be God; I do not want to be first among you. I want to make something beautiful. My fingers itch, perpetually, to touch and shape and mold. I wire and plumb and saw and paint and tune-up and weld, from the same instinct that called me to teach. There is ego in it, of course. But as God is my witness, I take the same divine pleasure in seeing the beautiful made by someone else as by me—in fact, more so, because of my own work I know so completely its flaws.

You should know then that my war with the world (and with myself—and sometimes with you) is a war against junk. Because junk is illusion and the creation of illusion, because junk robs us, finally, of our most precious capacity: the power to praise, and the deepening enjoyment of the truly good, God himself. To accept the necessity of making junk for any reason at all is to accept hell, and I cannot bear it.

And is it true, after all, that one person's junk is another's beauty? If you have understood me to be writing about my own snobbish taste, a Pecksniffian estheticism, then I have written badly. We all come equipped from childhood with culturally imposed preferences. Some like Van Gogh, others Paul Klee. Some like H. H. Richardson, others Frank Lloyd Wright. But almost everyone, within his own circle of experience, knows and recognizes quality, even if he cannot define it, and even if, in trapped hopelessness, he fails to serve it. For the Word has become flesh, full of glory, and testifies.

And testifies! Not what we say we are, but what they see we are. Faith and learning meet, if they meet anywhere, in flesh, which does not lie, and which, in its most perfect form, had finally to be committed to the cross. This may be our controlling paradigm—the apparent defeat, but the final triumph of the craftsman. "In my flesh," writes St. Paul, "shall I see God." Worthy flesh indeed! And if his tents leaked?

I want to be remembered as an honest craftsman, one who worked well and truly and with a whole heart. If this is not to be the truth about me, and if you are to be my faithful colleagues, you owe it to me above everything else to see to my amendment. For not to care enough about me to attempt my correction in this, exposes you to the same divine complaint. I know from experience how willing you are to forgive my personal and temperamental failures, and I thank you for that. It is in the essential where forgiving silence would be wrong.

Well then, what is my charter? Cut to the bone, I understand that I am charged to tell stories, and tell them well. Because I work in history, they must be true stories, as true as the evidence and critical judgment can make them, and they must be appealing, engaging the attention of my listeners for reasons of their own and enriching their understanding in ways not always apparent. As diligently as most, I have searched for some solution to history as satisfyingly elegant as the Pythagorean theorem or Newton's equation for gravity, for an abstraction, or a set of them, to untie the knot and bring a smooth order to view. Nor was it energy wasted. But I always found an inconvenient fact in the way, or a body of experience still outside, or (most difficult of all) came to a dull conclusion. Having arrived, I could not help wondering why I started out.

No: I came into the world crying for a story, and that is how I expect to leave it. The student who taught me this primal fact about myself had called History 191 "Uncle Zenos's Story Hour." Something in me (a bit of residual pomp) was a little hurt; yet he was a kindly fellow and meant it for a compliment. By degrees I have come to see the truth of it—the truth about what I was really doing, and the truth about the importance of story to the human condition.

From the beginning of my work, I have believed that the first need of a dimensional human being is memory, living memory. It is a matter both of head and of heart. Without the head, we have mere anecdote, pleasant enough, but without power. Without the heart, we have abstraction—power without context, a danger to humanity. Living memory begins when in some mysterious way the deathly veil is drawn aside, allowing us to witness a life, now gone, in its fullness. It is not enough to say in passing, "these bones were once a man." The man himself must stand forth, like Lazarus from his tomb, before we can know what it is to be human. For the man himself is more than we can say about him and to hold him in a living memory is to enlarge ourselves.

This is not a quarrel with abstraction, with science. We have no end of need for it; I applaud its progress and celebrate its victories. I say only that beyond science lies the bewilderingly profuse concreteness of what it studies, as lies the New Testament far beyond the best and most comprehensive propositions about it. I turn to science whenever it can serve me reliably, for a vaccine, an actuarial prediction, a dwell-meter, a phonograph. But for my moments of ultimate concern, I return again and again to a handful of stories: Eden, Abraham and Isaac, Bethlehem, Golgotha, the wrath of Achilles, the death of Socrates, the founding of

Plymouth Plantation, Pickett's charge. And I remember, almost word for word, the marvelous adventures of two brothers named Flip and Flop, for these were the stories mother told us as we lay in bed, waiting for sweet sleep.

I have been tempted to make Faust's demand—the power to sweep Caesar himself onto the stage, or Lincoln. But the price was too great. One cannot finally view reality by an instrument of illusion. For story is not illusion. It is a complex, subtle, demanding (and finally simple and effortless) vehicle to carry us there, where reality is. The requirements for great stories are awesome, beyond the powers of all but a handful of poets and historians. One must somehow have been there! I do not delude myself; in the company of Herodotus, Homer, Henry Adams, and Sam Morison, I am at best a raw apprentice. That does not trouble me. It is a joy to be permitted to sit in a corner of the shop, copying out the great themes, and allowed a minor exercise of my own, occasionally.

It is particularly required of me as a teacher that the stories I tell be suited to my listeners. The right story carries to the right listener a great weight of meaning, so great indeed that one may not suspect its full import until a long life's end. I have seen a persuasive argument that the story from which Shakespeare finally carved Hamlet was an expression of ancient distress at the observed precession of the equinox (Georgio di Santilliana, *Hamlet's Mill*). How many times have I heard "the time's out of joint" without a suspicion of that? And was it not rich otherwise? Indeed, but richer now, and each time repeated, for you will all remember how enhanced was your childlike pleasure in going over and over the same story, changed in nothing, not a syllable, yet each time, a subtly new experience. Are we then so far removed from childhood's need, for all our gray and creaky age?

My colleagues: remember that I am making confession, not argument. We have had our arguments through the years (and none more vigorous than with my colleagues in history); yet none of you has attempted to bar my way, and I have lived with the hope that whatever mischief I might thoughtlessly do could be corrected in another class, another conversation, by one of you. Just now a young lady, staggered by a brutal family tragedy, has said to me, "In some of my classes, I have seen how determined we are. In your class, I saw that I am free." She recognizes that both conditions are in some sense true, and I believe she sees that to struggle with that antinomy is a path to maturity.

This, then, is a kind of answer to the question: "How have you done in changing students?" How well I have done is honestly difficult to judge, for I can speak only of those who trouble themselves to return. They speak about the stories, and if their conversation shows enlarged human beings, how can I appropriate the virtue of it to something I have done? And as for those who remain silent, what does that mean? I confess with a sudden sense of shame that I have remained as silent to the author of some of the most magnificent lectures I have ever heard as to the perpetrator of the worst. No, I must take refuge in ignorance, except for my conviction, almost a priori, that a well-told story ought to make a difference.

Yet there is an area of discontent about the future that needs to be expressed here. My students have been remarkably forgiving people, too much so for my good. Many years have gone, legends have accumulated, images fixed. Occasionally a student will object, "but that is not what you said last year." I feel in them a powerful inertial force working against change in me, a kind of gyroscopic stubbornness in behalf of what they expect. It worries me, for though learning requires some orderliness of process, it also needs open spaces and fresh winds.

Beside, I have been increasingly skeptical of my effect in helping to create new storytellers. It does look as though old patterns need to be broken up—my old patterns, among others. The new distributions in the history program may now push me along in useful ways. The surveys will require changes in focus and scope, while the seminars will emphasize listening rather than telling. Somewhere in these new corridors may be a door to a new room where an old reptile can go to shed a skin or two.

I have spoken of craftsmanship and storytelling; you will have sensed their internal connection in my life. I wish now to speak briefly about community and my feelings about it.

For me, as for David Nyvall, North Park has always been a family matter, a tribal matter. I have taught happily, if briefly, elsewhere, but it was always to this little patch of ground that my heart was drawn. It is here that I have stood in the powerful and satisfying intersection of church, family, work, and friendship, here in this polis sheltered beneath the cupola. In the chaos of Robert Redfield's rampaging technical order, all surrounding and sometimes all but engulfing, this apparently frail but really tough little enclave has maintained itself, sustained and sustaining, through the decades. To its life, tens of thousands have contributed and have taken meaning from it in return. For all its faults, and I know them as well as anyone, the North Park community is my anchor and my shield, and to this day I think of my call to teach here as an act of gracious providence.

And that is why I have so often plagued your lives with what must seem an intolerable meddlesomeness. Athenians made it law that citizens who refused to take sides be fined for incivility. The true citizens were expected to be fair judges of public policy, and this in turn required of them that they be persons of broad experience and capacity. They had to have *arete*, well-rounded excellence. The story is told of an envious Greek from an insignificant polis, that he braced Themistocles with these words: "Themistocles, had you not been born a Athenian you would have come to nothing." The statesman replied, "That is quite true. And had you been born in Athens you would still have come to nothing."

What I am is partly what I do, but partly, inescapably, what you do. No action can be understood fully except in its context, a thing done in one part of a polis involves the whole polis. That is what community means, a web of interconnecting relationships such that to pluck a part of the web sets the whole in motion. It is from that perspective that I have so often, so angrily, rejected the contention that only specialists are qualified to judge a program, a policy.

I think, though, that I do not really fear the effect of our arguments on the life of the community. What worries me is our silences. More than anything else I have needed from my colleagues a serious, continuing, and demanding conversation about first questions. Lately, I have come to a sympathetic understanding of Harold Reever's shout to me across the street, "Zenos, what caused World War I?" Is it that I am too much across the street to many of you? Or is the silence an impersonal affliction, an operational fatigue arising from busyness and much striving after wind? Or is the absence of clear integrating commitments causing this drift apart, each into one's own household, reducing conversation to mere negotiation?

Surely it is the silences at work in many of the failures that depress me—our frequent lapses as generous hosts, our inability to gather ourselves for significant events, much less our failure to mobilize the whole body for moments of celebration, our difficulty with finding visible ways of recognizing excellence among our students, our inability to provide the same warmth and acceptance to off-campus as to on-campus students.

The world around us is fragmented into a myriad of specialties, the people in it torn between sacred and secular, scientific and humane, technical and organic. They hardly know themselves, so diverse and mutually conflicting are their various images. If what we are, at last, is what sells, we are condemned to eternal anxiety, for who can know tomorrow's market in a careening world?

Let us, instead, address seriously the deeps within us, searching not for what sells today, but for that which has always been and must always be the permanent concern of humankind. That is the spirit of our roots, and it has sustained us until now. It is quality that will save us, if we are to be saved in any meaningful sense, because quality was God's intention when he made the world. In that recognition, I am entirely at peace.